WASHINGTON COVER-UP

WASHINGTON COVER-UP

Clark R. Mollenhoff

DOUBLEDAY & COMPANY, INC., GARDEN CITY, NEW YORK

1962

CONTENTS

WASHINGTON COVER-UP

CHAPTER I

Secrecy Solves No Problems

No single factor is more important to the strength of our democracy than the free flow of accurate information about the government's operations. The citizen in a democracy must know what his government is doing, or he will lack the soundest basis for judging the candidates and the platforms of our political parties.

Our elected officials are given only a temporary grant of power, and only a temporary custody of government property and government records. Neither the President nor those he appoints have any royal prerogative; they have only a limited right to steer our government within the framework of the Constitution and the laws.

It is well to remember that every withholding of government business from the public is an encroachment upon the democratic principle that government officials are accountable to the people. It follows that citizens should regard all governmental secrecy with some suspicion as an encroachment on their right to know.

The American citizen should reject all arbitrary claims to secrecy by the bureaucracy as sharply as he would reject any claims to a right of the executive branch to by-pass Congress in levying taxes. A wise citizen should be as outraged at arbitrary secrecy as he would be at arbitrary imprisonment. Logically he should insist on the same safeguards against arbitrary secrecy that he would against unjustified arrest or taxation. The public's "right to know" is that basic.

Unfortunately, there is a general tendency to regard government secrecy as only a problem for the newspapers. And even within the newspaper profession there is a tendency to ignore government secrecy until it interferes with a story the individual reporter or editor wants to develop.

I am not interested in pleading for any special right of access to government information for newspapers or reporters. As vital as their function is, newspapers, magazines, television and radio for the most part merely provide an orderly process for disseminating information about government to the people who do not have the time, money, or technical facility to acquire the information for themselves. Transmitting information gathered at a government press conference or through a government press release does not necessarily answer the people's right to know.

The public has a right to expect that its government's press releases will be factually accurate, and for the most part they are. We also have a right to expect our highest officials to be factually accurate, but we must recognize realistically that it is only normal for them to color facts with opinions and conclusions that are most favorable to the political party in power.

This manipulation, shading, twisting, or omission of facts —often referred to as "managing the news"—will be limited only by the political fear of being exposed for having made erroneous or intentionally misleading statements to the public. As reprehensible as the practice can be, it is nevertheless a political fact of life and those who lament its existence would do better to bolster the one sure safeguard against it: the people's right to know—through the press and through their elected representatives in Congress. News management, I repeat, can be controlled only by insisting on the public's right to go behind the statements distributed by the government agencies or by high government officials.

Those who manipulate the news or try to cover their tracks with arbitrary secrecy are not likely to be pursuing totalitarian goals. Usually the only motivation is short-term political gain. Often it is rationalized on grounds that a few factual errors and overdrawn conclusions are not important when viewed in the total context of the achievements of the party in power. There is also the standard rationalization that a few distortions only serve to balance the distortions of the other political party.

No administration enjoys admitting errors or mismanagement of government. Because the criticism is usually initiated by the political opposition, it is often harsh and overdrawn. An instinctive defensiveness springs up within the defending political party, and the battle rages.

In the classic political controversy, the initial criticism has been followed by a demand for a full investigation. The press has already done some investigative work and has printed stories dealing with all available aspects of the controversy. However, when the probing by the press or by private citizens has not been conclusive, the Congress, throughout the history of the United States, has launched investigations to dig out the facts not otherwise available to the press or the public. And almost as often as the Congress has dug in, the executive branch has refused or been reluctant to co-operate.

A truly thorough investigation of the executive branch can be conducted only in the Congress. It is unreasonable to believe that an Attorney General, appointed by the President, will aggressively delve into an investigation of matters that might embarrass his own administration. For this reason, the right of the public and the press to government information is for the most part contingent upon the power of Congress to obtain documents and testimony from the executive branch.

If the committees of Congress, acting within the scope of

their authority, cannot obtain access to all the facts on government activity, then the facts can be arbitrarily hidden for the duration of the administration's power. Who would argue that any administration should be allowed to bury its crimes, its mismanagement, and its errors until a public, barred from full facts on these matters, decides to vote that party from power? Such a philosophy would put a premium on the Washington cover-up.

Properly authorized committees must have the power to compel government officials to testify and produce government records. If this power is lacking, the Congress, the press, and the public are dependent upon the information or half-information that the executive branch chooses to release. It should be obvious to even a novice in politics that politicians are not likely to voluntarily produce testimony or records that may harm their own aspirations.

Most congressional requests for information have been filled without trouble. The executive branch has resisted, however, whenever it seemed likely that congressional hearings would expose some political favorite or embarrass the administration. Invariably it has been claimed that the Congress was invading the executive branch and that some constitutional issue was involved.

In this book I will show how the executive branch, beginning with George Washington's administration, has handled requests from Congress for delivery of information. And I will show how the tendency to withhold information has grown, particularly since World War II.

It is not my intention to argue that all government information should be made public immediately, for I am fully aware of the need for security on military matters as well as the need for some restrictions on release of information from personnel files and investigative files.

In practice, we must allow our elected officials the right to withhold some kinds of information from the public. War plans and other papers involving military security are the more obvious examples. But any withholding should be done under specific grants of authority from Congress or under specific grants in the Constitution, and the authority should be carefully limited. The broad right of arbitrary withholding of information is not something that any officials should be permitted to arrogate to themselves.

There is ample justification for laws that set out areas of military information to be withheld from the general public. There always has been. It would be especially foolhardy in these days of serious international tension to insist on a full public disclosure of our military posture. However, this does not mean that all persons outside the military establishment should be barred from access to military information. There should be no question about proper committees of Congress having access to nearly all information on military spending, for this is the only way the Congress can obtain sufficient information for passing laws and appropriating money. Also, the auditors of the General Accounting Office (GAO) must have access to all but the most highly classified Defense secrets, or they will be unable to carry out their duties of determining whether expenditures are being made in an efficient and lawful manner.

There might also be justification for withholding information from the public when it involves diplomatic negotiations with a foreign nation. However, barring the public should not bar the GAO or properly authorized committees of Congress except under the most unusual and most clearly delineated circumstances.

There are other areas of government in which secrecy is justified. These include the raw investigative files of the Federal Bureau of Investigation (FBI), and some parts of the government personnel files. There are clear reasons for barring the public from the FBI investigative files, for these files contain much unevaluated rumor and many unauthenticated documents. Also, as FBI Director J. Edgar Hoover has pointed out, much mischief could be done by the underworld and subversive elements if they had access to FBI files.

But while we are using a limited secrecy to guard our chief federal investigative agency, we must realize that law enforcement agencies can go wrong if there is not some regular scrutiny from the outside. This was demonstrated in the twenties, just prior to the time when J. Edgar Hoover was put in charge of cleaning up the federal investigative agency. We have been fortunate to have a J. Edgar Hoover heading the FBI, but we cannot assume that the office will always be filled by one whose major ambition is creating and maintaining a skilled career investigative agency.

Under unusual circumstances, arrangements have been made for examination of an entire FBI file by the chairmen of the Judiciary committees of the House and Senate. On occasion, the ranking minority member of these committees has taken part. Since this procedure provides for examination by a Democrat and a Republican, it has the strength of being bipartisan. It has the disadvantage of depending on the character and personality of the majority and minority representatives for true bipartisanship. The procedure is a touchy one that the press, the public, and the Congress must scrutinize periodically. Certainly the FBI must have a right to keep its files secret from the public, but it should never be forgotten that some limited bipartisan congressional group must have authority to examine these files if we are to remain secure from possible abuse of power.

President Truman wrapped government personnel files in secrecy on the theory that making them available to a Republican-dominated committee of Congress could result in the use of rumor and hearsay to "smear" government officials. Certainly it is laudable to try to protect government employees from baseless charges. But this "protection" for the government employees has its drawbacks. Such secrecy has been used to prevent government employees from gaining access to their own medical records which were material to a defense in an ouster action. It also shields government personnel administrators from criticism and thereby encourages arbitrary actions.

I learned once of a case in which the secrecy surrounding personnel files made it impossible for a woman to find out why she had been discharged by the government. I will refer to the woman as Mrs. A, for there is no necessity of stirring up more problems for her now if she has been able to find a job after being out of work for several years.

Mrs. A was a woman of about fifty with more than twenty years of service with the Civil Service Commission as a shorthand reporter. She had had some problems with an employee in the same section and some disagreement with a supervisor. She was asked to go to the Department of Health, Education and Welfare for a physical examination.

Mrs. A took the physical examination and shortly afterwards was forced to resign. She was given no reason except that something in the physical examination made her unqualified to continue as a government employee. Mrs. A went to a private physician and had a thorough examination to try to find out why she was unqualified to hold her job with the government. The doctor could find no reason for her discharge.

At this point Mrs. A hired a lawyer. Neither the doctor nor the lawyer could obtain access to the records of the physical examination given to Mrs. A at the Department of Health, Education and Welfare. The lawyer hired by Mrs. A found himself tilting with a ghost. He could not find out why his client was discharged, and yet he was faced with trying to establish proof that whatever was alleged was not true.

I could not believe the story Mrs. A told when she first

came to my office, but I said I would examine it and see what I could do. It checked out in every detail. I was informed at the Health, Education and Welfare Department that the physical records of all government employees were confidential. There were no exceptions. I pointed out that this confidential status was set up for the purpose of protecting the government employees against public intrusion, but that it certainly couldn't be meant to keep a government employee or her private doctor from examining her records. Officials at the Department of Health, Education and Welfare disagreed. I made repeated calls to see if I could get the policy changed, but to no avail.

Mrs. A was a little more distressed each time she came by the office, for I was unable to interest anyone in her case. She was not important. She was not the center of a big political drama.

Was it a wrongful discharge? I could not answer the question when it was raised by lawyers for committees of Congress. It was possible the file would have shown justifiable grounds for the discharge. I could only argue that it was wrong to bar this woman, her lawyer, and her doctor from examination of a file giving the results of her government health examination.

Despite the inequity in this case and others similar to it, a general belief prevailed in Washington that secrecy on government personnel files and loyalty-security files was an unmixed blessing. The fallacy of this contention was impressed on me every time I saw Mrs. A. She was defeated in appearance, and she was deeply hurt.

There is a sharp cruelty in secrecy that results in such injury to an individual, and there is great damage to our government—and to people's faith in it—when secrecy is used to cover up mismanagement and corruption. I am gravely concerned over any obstructions put in the way of congressional committees' investigating the abuses of secrecy. Where would we be if Congress had not looked into such nefarious schemes as the Teapot Dome scandals of the Harding administration or the tax "fixes" in the Truman administration?

Have we, a self-governing people, learned anything from these black marks on our history? I am afraid that we have not learned enough yet. I am afraid that the people as a whole, and many persons in the press and Congress, tend to disregard the danger signs and accept the self-serving declarations of virtue from their Presidents or other high officials. A few newspapers, a few diligent investigators for congressional committees, a few senators and a few congressmen have had to take the whole responsibility for breaking through unjustified secrecy and uncovering the truth.

In my twenty years as a newspaper correspondent I have been concerned with this problem of information policies at every level of government—starting in a local police station, city hall, county courthouse, and state capitol. For the past eleven years I have been covering the federal government for the Washington Bureau of Cowles Publications. I have been fortunate to have the freedom to follow any investigations that interested me, as well as the enthusiastic support of several newspapers. My position has afforded me the privilege of a day-to-day acquaintanceship with every major investigation in Washington since 1950.

The problem of the Washington cover-up became a major interest to me in connection with the scandals in the Reconstruction Finance Corporation (RFC) and the Internal Revenue Service beginning in 1950. The investigations of the RFC were of a reasonably short duration. The pattern of "political favoritism" in administering this government loaning agency was ended when W. Stuart Symington, later a United States Senator, was named by President Truman to restore order. Symington instituted the "fishbowl policy" that brought most of the RFC operations out in the open.

The problems with secrecy in the Internal Revenue Service remained a major news story for more than two years. The Internal Revenue law provides that it is unlawful to disclose the information on the tax returns submitted by U.S. taxpayers. It was a secrecy established in a specific statute, and the purpose was to protect the privacy of the finances of individual taxpayers. However, investigations by Senator John J. Williams, the Delaware Republican, and a House subcommittee, headed by Representative Cecil King, the California Democrat, showed that the secrecy was used to shield crooked tax agents and tax collectors from exposure and prosecution.

The Alcohol Tax Unit (ATU), a division of the Internal Revenue Service, had even set up procedures to provide for secret settlements of criminal law violations. Also, ATU provided secret hearings on applications for a federal license to wholesale liquor or beer. A racketeer found it possible to go into a secret hearing, give perjured testimony, and obtain a license with the help of weak or corrupt ATU administrators.

The lesson was clear in each case: secrecy corrupts. It allowed government officials to dispense favors behind closed doors. When decisions were secret, there was no need to provide any consistency in decisions or in penalties. It was impossible for the public or the press to obtain enough information to register an informed objection.

During fights to open records in the Internal Revenue Service, I became acquainted with James S. Pope, executive editor of the Louisville *Courier-Journal* who was then chairman of the Freedom of Information Committee of the American Society of Newspaper Editors. We worked together in forcing the Internal Revenue Service to open certain "compromise settlements" of tax cases as well as the ATU hearings.

In exploring these and other information problems, I worked closely with the late Harold Cross, former special counsel for the American Society of Newspaper Editors; J. Russell Wiggins, executive editor of the Washington *Post and Times Herald;* Herbert Brucker, editor of the Hartford *Courant;* and V. M. (Red) Newton, managing editor of the Tampa *Tribune.*

We shared a deep suspicion of government secrecy and also resented what it did in corrupting our system of government. I was privileged to serve as a member of the national Freedom of Information Committee of Sigma Delta Chi (the journalism fraternity) and handle the Washington phase of the reports for Red Newton for a period of more than five years. For a longer period I have worked with the American Society of Newspaper Editors' Freedom of Information Committee. I have testified before committees of the House and Senate.

My testimony before the Moss subcommittee in November 1955 was the first testimony on the scope of the problem of "executive privilege" advanced by the Eisenhower administration. I have kept in touch continuously with Representative John Moss, the California Democrat, and the members of his staff from the time their subcommittee was established. I am particularly indebted to Staff Administrator Sam Archibald, Staff Consultant Paul Southwick, and staff lawyers John Mitchell and the late Jacob Scher.

Others who were particularly helpful and co-operative over these years were the late Senator Thomas Hennings (Dem., Mo.); Charles Slayman, counsel for the Hennings Judiciary Subcommittee; Senator John McClellan (Dem., Ark.), and Robert F. Kennedy, who was his chief counsel; Herbert Maletz, chief counsel for a House Judiciary Subcommittee; Representative Porter Hardy (Dem., Va.); John Reddan, chief counsel for the Hardy Government Operations Subcommittee; Representative F. Edward Hebert (Dem., La.); James Naughton, chief counsel for the Fountain Government Operations Subcommittee; and John Courtney, chief counsel for the Hebert Armed Services Subcommittee; Arthur John Keefe, counsel for the Senate Antitrust and Monopoly Subcommittee; and Representative George Meader (Rep., Mich.).

The knowledge of the secrecy problem gained by most of these lawmakers and lawyers has been understandably confined to their experiences with one or two committees, whereas I have had the opportunity to become aware of the day-to-day activities of nearly all the committees. For that reason, and because of my alarm at the public apathy over government secrecy, I have decided to set the whole story down in one place. Most of the story is taken from the official records of congressional committees—the sworn testimony, the correspondence with government agencies, and the official reports of Senate and House investigators. As much as possible, I have put it together in chronological, narrative form so that the reader may discover, as I did, how the abuse of government secrecy has spread and just how vast and serious the scope of it has become. At the end of the book I will make some recommendations that I hope may serve as a guide to eliminating this serious threat to our democratic form of government.

CHAPTER II

The First Century

An Indian uprising along the Indiana-Ohio border in 1791 set the stage for the first investigation by Congress of decisions in the executive branch. President Washington, then in his first term, sent Major General Arthur St. Clair into the wilderness to put a stop to the raids.

General St. Clair and his fourteen hundred American soldiers were camped along the headwaters of the Wabash River on November 3 when they were surprised by the attack of a strong force led by Little Turtle, chief of the Miami.

The Indians killed more than six hundred officers and men and forced the others to retreat. It was a humiliating defeat, one that still ranks among the worst in our history. Congress demanded an explanation.

On March 27, 1792, the House of Representatives appointed a select committee to inquire into the failure of the St. Clair expedition, and "to call for such persons, papers, and records, as may be necessary to assist their inquiries." For the first time, the President and his Cabinet were presented with the problem of whether to make papers and testimony available to Congress.

President Washington called a meeting of his full Cabinet to determine the proper way to proceed, for he was aware that the action taken would set a precedent on such matters.

Thomas Jefferson wrote the following account of the meeting and the conclusions drawn by the Washington Cabinet:

"First, that the House was an inquest, and therefore might institute inquiries. Second, that it might call for papers generally. Third, that the Executive ought to communicate such papers as the public good would permit, and ought to refuse those, the disclosure of which would injure the public; consequently were to exercise a discretion. Fourth, that neither the committee nor House had a right to call on the head of a department, who and whose papers were under the President alone; but that the committee should instruct their chairman to move the House to address the President."

Jefferson also wrote:

"Hamilton agreed with us in all these points except as to the power of the House to call on the heads of departments. He observed that as to his department, the act constituting it had made it subject to Congress in some points, but he thought himself not so far subject as to be obliged to produce all the papers they might call for. They might demand secrets of a very mischievous nature. (Here I thought he began to fear they would go on to examining how far their own members and other persons in the government had been dabbling in stocks, banks, etc., and that he probably would choose in this case to deny their power; and in short, he endeavored to place himself subject to the House, when the Executive should propose what he did not like, and subject to the Executive when the House should propose anything disagreeable.) . . . Finally agreed, to speak separately to the members of the committee, and bring them by persuasion into the right channel. It was agreed in this case, that there was not a paper which might not be properly produced; that if they should desire it, a clerk should attend with the originals to be verified by themselves."

Although the Cabinet indicated a need for a discretion to withhold papers "which would injure the public," President Washington agreed that in the case of the St. Clair expedition "there was not a paper which might not be produced."

There was no withholding by President Washington in this case, and it could hardly be regarded seriously as a precedent for any right to arbitrarily refuse executive papers to Congress.

There was one other instance in Washington's administration in which the Congress asked for executive papers. In this case, the House of Representatives asked for the papers and instructions to United States ambassadors who negotiated the Jay treaty. This time Washington refused to deliver the papers to the House on the specific constitutional grounds that the Senate, not the House, is authorized to advise and consent on treaty matters.

A Supreme Court case in the administration of President Thomas Jefferson raised the question of whether it was possible for the courts to force the Cabinet to perform certain acts required by law. In the last hours of the administration of President John Adams a "midnight appointment" was made of a justice of the peace for the District of Columbia named William Marbury, a minor Federalist political figure. James Madison, who became the new Secretary of State in the Jefferson administration, refused to deliver the commission to Marbury to complete the appointment process.

Marbury asked the Supreme Court to issue a writ of mandamus under the Judiciary Act of 1789 to force Madison to deliver the commission. In February 1803, Chief Justice John Marshall delivered the opinion of the court. First he dealt with the question of whether Madison had a right to refuse to deliver the commission to a properly appointed official. The decision was a rebuke to Secretary of State Madison and stated: "Is it to be contended that the heads of departments are not amenable to the laws of their country?"

However, the opinion went on to conclude that the Constitution provided no method for the Supreme Court to issue writs to force the executive action requested. Chief Justice

Marshall stated that the Judiciary Act providing for a writ was inconsistent with the Constitution, and that "a law repugnant to the Constitution is void."

Although Madison was wrong in withholding the commission from Marbury, the court held that under the Constitution there was no way to force action. The case did not mean that Madison had a legal right, but only that Marbury had no remedy. The Marbury appointment was in essence a political matter and could only have been countered indirectly by the impeachment of the President.

The specific question of congressional access to executive papers was raised in one case in the Jefferson administration. In 1807, President Jefferson was requested to furnish the House "any information in the possession of the Executive" on the allegation of a conspiracy by Aaron Burr. However, the request specifically exempted papers "such as he [Jefferson] may deem the public welfare to require not to be disclosed."

President Jefferson displayed an awareness of the dangers of arbitrary withholding of information by carefully explaining the nature of the papers he did not deliver. He stated that these papers included matters "chiefly in the form of letters, often containing such a mixture of rumors, conjectures, and suspicions as to render it difficult to sift out the real facts and unadvisable to hazard more than general outlines, strengthened by concurrent information or the particular credibility of the relator."

Later, when Aaron Burr was actually tried for treason in Richmond, Chief Justice Marshall issued a subpoena for papers in Jefferson's custody, including a private letter from General James Wilkinson to Jefferson. While Jefferson continued to assert a right to determine which papers he would produce, he did in fact send all the documents requested in the subpoena. Also, General Wilkinson appeared at the trial and testified fully about his communications with President

Jefferson. Chief Justice Marshall's decision conceded that the President could not be summoned to make a personal appearance before a judicial body because of the nature of his position and the dignity of his office. Since Jefferson produced all the documents under subpoena there was no need for adjudicating the issue of what types of papers might be withheld. [The trial eventually resulted in a jury acquittal for Burr.]

Until President Jackson's term there were no significant controversies over requests for information. Jackson was involved in a number of disputes. Although he consistently asserted a right to withhold information from Congress, he usually sent the requested documents along with his angry criticism of Congress for making the requests.

A Senate investigation of land frauds in the Jackson administration resulted in demands for papers dealing with land transactions conducted by a Jackson appointee. President Jackson refused to deliver the papers to Congress, but the resulting cover-up of land frauds could hardly be called a precedent worthy to be followed.

President John Tyler was requested to submit to the House of Representatives the reports of Lieutenant Colonel Ethan Allen Hitchcock concerning an investigation of frauds which were alleged to have been perpetrated on the Cherokee Indians. President Tyler produced a part of the information at the time of the request but declined to produce the full investigative reports in 1843. He argued that to be effective such investigations must often be confidential.

"They may result in the collection of truth or falsehood; or they may be incomplete, and may require further prosecution," Tyler said. "To maintain that the President can exercise no discretion . . . would deprive him at once of the means of performing one of the most salutary duties of his office . . . and would render him dependent upon . . . [another] branch [of government] in the performance of a duty purely executive."

However, in a later message to Congress on the Cherokee Indians matter, President Tyler directed that all of the reports be made available. He did not acknowledge the right of Congress to command the Executive to produce all information. Neither did he claim an unlimited right for the President to withhold. He declared that there must be some discretion left with the President when "the interests of the country or of individuals" is to be affected by production of the records. He enumerated some circumstances in which he felt the President actually had a duty to withhold—as, for example, during a pending law enforcement investigation.

After the Civil War there was a flurry of investigations, but these caused little conflict. The corrupters in the Grant administration were foresighted enough to bring key members of the Republican Congress into their dishonest schemes as an insurance against exposure by the committees of Congress.

A Democratic Congress, elected in 1874, initiated a series of investigations into the War and Treasury Departments to eradicate the corruption and to set the stage for the next presidential campaign in 1876. The frauds were so raw that the feeble efforts to hide them were useless. The inquiries disclosed how the government was defrauded by a "Whisky Ring" that evaded millions of dollars in taxes on distilled whisky. The "ring" operated with co-operation from some Treasury officials as well as from President Grant's private secretary, General Orville E. Babcock.

Another congressional investigation of the Grant administration implicated Secretary of War W. W. Belknap in widespread graft in the assignment of trading posts in the Indian territory. He resigned from office in the face of a threat of impeachment, carrying with him a presidential letter expressing "regret" that he was leaving government.

President Grant's letter of "regret" to a man who had betrayed a trust set a pattern for Presidents for a long time to come. The whole ritual, indeed, has remained the same. First come the accusations, followed by denials of any improprieties. Then comes the effort to hide the records. This is followed by the tardy admission of facts but a denial of illegality, and finally the letter from the President lauding the dishonest public official for his fine service coupled with "regretful" acceptance of his resignation.

The corruption of the Grant administration is considered by many to be the worst blot on the nation's escutcheon. Republican political figures organized a constuction firm, the Crédit Mobilier of America, which was used to divert lavish profits from the building of the Union Pacific Railway. An American diplomatic figure lent his name to a huge mine swindle, Navy contracts were for sale, and there were wholesale frauds in the custom houses.

The widespread scandals of the Grant administration presented no basic problem for Congress in obtaining government records because the key evidence in these cases could be obtained from sources outside the executive branch.

However, a problem did develop in 1876 when the Democratic House sought to obtain testimony and records of financial transactions of Jay Cooke & Company. Jay Cooke & Company was one of the largest financial institutions of the time, and Jay Cooke was close to the Grant administration and Republican party politics. When the House of Representatives discovered that the Secretary of the Treasury had deposited large sums of money with a London branch of Jay Cooke & Company, it sought to determine whether there was some impropriety involved in the decision to make the deposit.

In the course of its investigation, the House issued a subpoena for Hallet Kilbourn, who managed some real estate operations for Jay Cooke & Company. Kilbourn refused to produce the documents sought and argued that the House had no right to investigate private affairs. The House ordered him arrested for contempt.

Kilbourn was imprisoned by House Sergeant at Arms John Thompson. Kilbourn immediately obtained a court order for his release and then sued Thompson for false imprisonment. The U. S. Supreme Court held that Thompson was liable for damages, and in the decision threw a doubt over the right of Congress to punish witnesses for refusing to answer questions or produce records.

The decision upset the long-standing view that the power of Congress to investigate was as broad as the almost limitless power of inquiry of the British Parliament. The U. S. Supreme Court stated:

"We are sure no person can be punished for contumacy as a witness of either House, unless his testimony is required in a matter into which that House has jurisdiction to inquire, and we feel equally sure that neither of these bodies possess the general power of making inquiry into private affairs of the citizen."

It was not until 1927, when the U. S. Supreme Court decided the case of *McGrain v. Daugherty*, that the right of Congress to compel testimony was firmly reaffirmed. In the intervening thirty-five years two Presidents successfully resisted the Congress!

President Grover Cleveland, a Democrat, faced a Republican Senate, and Theodore Roosevelt, an independent-minded Republican, took delight in testing his strength even against a Republican Congress.

President Cleveland in 1886 backed his Attorney General in refusing to deliver to the Senate some reports dealing with the administration of the United States District Attorney's office in the District of Columbia. The man who had held the office had been suspended, and Cleveland argued that the report on the reasons was the business of the executive branch. Because the Kilbourn case had weakened the position of Congress, Cleveland was not challenged.

President Theodore Roosevelt refused to allow his Attorney General to deliver papers to the Senate dealing with the status of investigations involving the U.S. Steel Corporation. The papers included an Attorney General's opinion on the U.S. Steel Corporation case.

Although the papers sought involved a pending case, the Senate insisted on pursuing the matter. Herbert K. Smith, head of the Bureau of Corporations, was summoned and was threatened with contempt and imprisonment if he failed to produce the documents. President Roosevelt asked Smith for the papers and, after taking them into his possession, informed the Senate the only way they could get the papers would be by impeaching him. The Senate then dropped the matter.

The infamous scandals of the Harding administration renewed the will of the Congress, and proved for all time the need for Congress to investigate even when a President assures the public that "all is well."

CHAPTER III

Teapot Dome to the Tax Scandals

Before Congress completed its investigations of the Harding administration scandals, cabinet officers had been found to be involved in the maladministration or corruption. Secretary of Navy Edwin Denby resigned from office under a barrage of criticism. Attorney General Harry M. Daugherty, involved in several questionable financial transactions, was indicted on a charge of having accepted a $200,000 payoff in connection with handling of Alien Property Custodian affairs. Daugherty was acquitted of the criminal charge, but reports of Congress established him as corrupt and incompetent in the handling of his office. Secretary of Interior Albert Fall was convicted of accepting a bribe and sent to prison.

It was in May 1921, within a year of President Harding's election, that Secretary of Interior Fall persuaded the President and Navy Secretary Denby to transfer certain naval oil reserves from the Navy to the Interior Department. Once he got them within his domain, Fall then transferred the oil reserves—at Teapot Dome, Wyoming, and Elk Hills, California—to two private oil producers, Harry Sinclair and E. L. Doheny. The leases were signed secretly, without competitive bidding, and Secretary of Interior Fall conveniently tossed them into a drawer away from public view. He then proceeded to collect $100,000 from Doheny for the Elk Hills transfer, and $300,000 from Sinclair for the Teapot Dome transfer.

Months later when the Democrats learned of the oil leases they demanded explanations and alleged, without substantiation, that the leases might involve some improprieties. Fall and Denby explained that the transfers to the Interior Department and the leasings were "in the public interest."

When President Harding put his personal stamp of approval on the leasing of the oil reserves, public sentiment turned against the investigating Democrats. A big, smiling man with an open face that seemed to project total integrity, Harding easily gave the impression that all was well with the oil reserve transactions. Although events later proved that he lacked understanding of the Teapot Dome scandals as well as many other important matters that took place in his administration, his reassurances at this stage were readily accepted by the public and the press.

Nevertheless, the Senate investigating committee persisted. Both Secretary of Interior Fall and Secretary of Navy Denby were called to testify. It was essential to question these two high-level government officials to lay the groundwork for the investigation. It was essential to explore the conversations between them, as well as the personal financial transactions between Fall and the Doheny and Sinclair interests. It was also necessary to explore the opinions and recommendations of subordinate officials.

Without all of this information, Congress could not have proved the dishonest use of a government position by Albert Fall. It would have been naïve to expect that the Justice Department under Harry Daugherty would have conducted an investigation that was fair and objective, for Daugherty was already mired in his own corruption.

The Harding scandals should have demonstrated for all time that the public cannot rely on any administration to police itself. Nor can it rely on the self-serving declarations of a President, however well-meaning he may be.

President Harding died on August 2, 1923, a broken and disillusioned man, still unaware, however, of the full extent of the scandals. Coolidge's administration and most of Hoover's had passed before the investigations were finally completed, the convictions recorded, the appeals completed, and Fall imprisoned in 1931.

President Coolidge was faced with a request for a list of the companies in which his Secretary of Treasury, Andrew Mellon, had an interest. A special Senate investigating committee was studying the Bureau of Internal Revenue and wanted to investigate the tax returns of firms with which Mellon was associated.

President Coolidge said it would be "detrimental to the public service" to reveal the list of Mellon's business interests and the tax returns of those firms. With that, the investigation ended.

Another request for information was similarly nipped by Hoover. The Senate Foreign Relations Committee had requested that Secretary of State Henry L. Stimson produce the contents of telegrams and letters leading up to the London Conference and the London Treaty. The committee contended it had a special right to such papers because of the constitutional prerogative of the Senate in the treaty-making process. Stimson disagreed and President Hoover backed him, arguing that in order to maintain friendly relations with other nations, it would be unwise to give the Senate all of the information on statements leading up to the treaty.

President Franklin D. Roosevelt was favored with a Congress that was largely on his side in his first two terms, so that there were no conflicts over information sought by Congress. Indeed, President Roosevelt preferred having committees of Congress investigate and dramatize problems in order to facilitate the passage of various New Deal measures.

Congress did run into opposition to requests for information in Roosevelt's third term, however. In 1941 Roosevelt rejected requests for FBI records and reports, and in 1944 FBI Director J. Edgar Hoover refused to testify or to give Congress a copy of a presidential directive requiring him, in the interests of national security, to refrain from testifying.

The President was backed by a ruling from his Attorney General, Francis Biddle. In a letter dated January 22, 1944, Biddle claimed that communications between the President and the heads of departments were confidential and privileged and not subject to inquiry by Congress. Another opinion by the Attorney General had previously supported President Roosevelt in refusing to make records of the Bureau of the Budget available to Congress.

The Roosevelt administration also used the secrecy routine to hamper a House investigation of the Federal Communications Commission (FCC) in 1943 and 1944. The FCC probe involved the basic charge of political tampering with an independent regulatory agency. There were indications of improper secret contacts with some commission members while cases were being decided.

The Roosevelt administration used every political method available to impede the investigations, including the use of friends in Congress to harass the investigators. Two men who successively held the title of general counsel—Eugene L. Garey and John J. Sirica—resigned in the face of the obstructions and harassment. They charged the investigation was being turned into a "whitewash."

The final report of the committee gave the FCC a clean bill of health. However, the minority report filed by Representative Richard B. Wigglesworth, Republican of Massachusetts, stated: "It has been impossible for the committee to conduct anything approaching a thoroughgoing investigation."

Congressman Wigglesworth charged that the committee

consistently acted "to suppress indefinitely alleged unsavory facts said to involve high administration officials and advisers." He made reference to the "methods both brutal and shameful" used to force the original chairman of the investigating committee to resign, and to the general atmosphere that resulted in the resignations of counsels Garey and Sirica.

The unhealthy conditions, which the House committee had started to expose, were left to fester, and fourteen years later the full effects burst on the American public. The investigations of the House Legislative Oversight Subcommittee in 1957, 1958, and 1959, which will be described in a later chapter, disclosed that the successful blocking of the FCC investigation in 1944 not only allowed bad practices to continue but thereby encouraged corruption.

Though President Roosevelt had directed the Secretaries of War and Navy not to deliver some documents which the FCC investigators had requested, his stated reason was simply that it would "not be in the public interest." No broad claims of a constitutional right to withhold information were ever invoked. There was no need for them because the cover-up was that ruthless and that effective. Had the nation not been at war, such a cover-up would likely have caused a major uproar.

The end of World War II and the election of a Republican Congress in 1946, however, brought the Democrats to heel. From the time the Republican Congress took control of the committees, the Truman administration was in almost constant combat with Congress. The first disputes involved the efforts of Republican committees of Congress to obtain access to FBI records and loyalty files. Later disputes centered on efforts to gain access to records of the Bureau of Internal Revenue and the Justice Department.

In 1947, the Republicans were intent on demonstrating that the Truman administration was "coddling Communists."

Investigators sought access to personnel records and letters dealing with the retention and promotion of persons who were alleged to be security risks or of questionable loyalty.

President Truman issued an executive order barring Congress from access to any of the loyalty or security information in the personnel files of the government. He said it was to protect the government employees from abuse by committees of Congress. The unrestrained activities of some congressional investigators did indeed make the order seem justifiable to many. However, the Republicans viewed it as a cover-up.

Representative Richard M. Nixon, later the Vice President, Representative Charles Halleck, later the Republican leader, and a dozen other prominent Republicans kept a continuous barrage of criticism firing at President Truman.

Said Representative Nixon on April 22, 1948:

"I say that this proposition cannot stand from a constitutional standpoint or on the basis of the merits for this very good reason: They would mean the President could have arbitrarily issued an Executive order in the [Bennett] Meyers case, the Teapot Dome case, or any other case denying the Congress of the United States information it needed to conduct an investigation of the Executive department and the Congress would have no right to question his decision."

Again, three years later, Representative Halleck was saying on the House floor:

"His [Truman's] censorship order gives every agency and department of the Government the absolute power to decide what information shall be kept from them. These agency heads are absolute czars unto themselves. When they order the iron curtain down it stays down—a gag on the press and radio of the nation."

Most of this initial criticism was aimed at the rather limited presidential order which barred Congress from the government personnel files in the investigations of loyalty and security cases.

Although the Truman administration was reluctant to make records available when the Republicans began looking into allegations of improper activities and political favoritism in the Reconstruction Finance Corporation (RFC), in the Bureau of Internal Revenue, and in the Justice Department, no blanket order was issued refusing testimony or records. The allegations were followed first by denials. Then there was stalling but finally, under the pressure of public opinion, the records were made available.

What happened specifically was this: Senator John J. Williams, the Delaware Republican, produced some fairly well documented cases of favoritism and bungling in the nation's number one tax agency. President Truman, Secretary of Treasury John Snyder, and Attorney General J. Howard McGrath all denied there was any widespread laxity or corruption in the administration of the federal tax laws. Daniel Bolich, the Assistant Commissioner of Internal Revenue, and T. Lamar Caudle, the Assistant Attorney General in charge of the Tax Division, went before the investigating committees and assured the leaders of Congress that all was well.

The self-serving declarations of the Truman administration did not satisfy Senator Williams, however, for they were inconsistent with many documented facts he held in his possession. A subcommittee of the House Ways and Means Committee was then established to conduct a deeper investigation into the handling of tax cases in the Bureau of Internal Revenue. Later a subcommittee of the House Judiciary Committee was organized to conduct some further examination of the way the Justice Department handled tax cases as well as other matters.

Because tax cases were handled by the Bureau of Internal Revenue, a branch of the Treasury Department, and prosecuted by the Justice Department, both departments were involved in the investigation. Tax cases, it was learned, could be fixed in their initial stages by Internal Revenue agents, or they could be sidetracked at higher levels in the Bureau of Internal Revenue; they could be rejected for prosecution by the Justice Department in Washington, or kicked aside by the United States District Attorney. There were at least a half-dozen points where a "fix" could take place, and congressional investigations disclosed that some cases were manipulated at almost all stages.

When at first the Justice Department files were not made available, the stalling was recognized for what it was—an effort to hide records that might be embarrassing. Newspapers quickly pointed out the cover-up, and Acting Attorney General Philip B. Perlman was forced to lay down procedural rules for the committees of Congress to use in requesting access to Justice Department files.

Perlman stated that the Justice Department would not give Congress access to open cases, but that closed files would be made available. He also said that FBI reports and similar confidential information would not be made available. The closed files and the testimony of high officials were nevertheless sufficient to enable Congress to document the record of the mishandling of federal tax investigations and prosecution. Congress extracted testimony from two cabinet officials—Attorney General J. Howard McGrath and Secretary of Treasury John Snyder. They revealed their conversations and communications with their highest subordinates. Records were produced showing the advice, recommendations, and conclusions of investigators in the Internal Revenue Service and the staff lawyers in the Justice Department. It was clear that some of the cases had not been handled in the normal manner, and that recommendations from subordinate officials were disregarded at some key points.

Only through this full examination was it possible to prove

that some cases were being "fixed" for money or for political considerations. Without the full record on the recommendations from lower officials it would have been impossible to prove that the mismanagement was due to anything more than "poor judgment" or negligence.

Neither Attorney General McGrath nor Treasury Secretary Snyder was shown to be involved in illegal tampering with any tax cases. However, they had contended that the initial allegations of fraud and mismanagement were untrue.

The investigations by Congress proved that several high officials were involved in outright fraud, and a good many more were involved in gross negligence. The Commissioner of Internal Revenue, the Assistant Commissioner, and the chief counsel for the Bureau of Internal Revenue all resigned under fire.

A former Commissioner of Internal Revenue, Joseph Nunan, was subsequently indicted and convicted on charges of failing to report large amounts of unexplained income. Assistant Commissioner Daniel Bolich was indicted and convicted on charges of failing to report more than $200,000 in income, though the conviction was later upset by the United States Supreme Court on technical grounds. T. Lamar Caudle, former Assistant Attorney General, in charge of the Tax Division, was indicted, convicted, and sent to prison on a criminal charge arising out of his mishandling of a federal income tax case. Convicted with Caudle was Matthew Connelly, appointment secretary for President Truman.

In total, dozens of tax officials were ousted from office for questionable handling of tax cases, and dozens were indicted and convicted on charges of cheating on their own tax returns. The mismanagement and fraud, which the Truman administration had sought to deny existed, was more widespread and sordid than most of the critics of the Bureau of Internal Revenue had imagined. The damage to the integrity of the nation's tax system was incalculable.

If ever a scandal were needed to prove the necessity of a congressional review to keep our big federal agencies open and clean, the Truman tax scandal was it. The success of their investigations only goaded the Republicans to further probing and policing. In their party platform of 1952, the Republicans pledged "to put an end to corruption, to oust the crooks and grafters, to administer tax laws fairly and impartially, and to restore honest government to the people."

When he accepted the party's nomination in Chicago on July 11, 1952, General Dwight D. Eisenhower said:

"Our aims—the aim of this Republican crusade—are clear: to sweep from office an Administration which has fastened on every one of us the wastefulness, the arrogance and corruption in high places, the heavy burdens and the anxieties which are the bitter fruit of a party too long in power."

"What the Washington mess must have is the full treatment," Candidate Eisenhower declared at Atlanta, Ga., on September 2, 1952. "The only clean-up that will do the job is the wholesale cleanout of the political bosses in Washington. I pledge you that . . . I shall not rest until the peddlers of privilege and the destroyers of decency are banished from the nation's house."

Two days later at Philadelphia, he spoke of the need for an open, frank government:

"We must not minimize the difficulties; neither can we seek with words and dollars to make the going look easy when it is tough. There will be mistakes, but the mistakes we make will not be doctored up to look like triumphs. There will be no curtain of evasion, of suppression, or double talk between ourselves and the people."

At Des Moines, Iowa, on September 18: "We are going to cast out the crooks and their cronies . . . And when it comes to casting out the crooks and their cronies, I can promise you that we won't wait for congressional prodding and investigations. The prodding this time will start from the top.

And when we are through, the experts in shady and shoddy government operations will be on their way back to the shadowy haunts, the sub-cellars of American politics from whence they came . . . The first thing we have to do is get a government that is honest. . . ."

And at St. Louis, Mo.:

". . . we must take the people, themselves, into our confidence and thereby, restore their confidence in government. We will keep the people informed because an informed people is the keystone in the arch of free government."

The crusade against secrecy and corruption stayed at the forefront of the campaign and swept Eisenhower and Nixon into office on November 4. When the electoral vote was tallied, it stood 422 Republicans to 89 Democrats—a genuine mandate to clean up "the mess in Washington."

CHAPTER IV

Army-McCarthy — A Claim of Secrecy Unlimited

On the morning of May 17, 1954, the klieg-lighted Senate Caucus Room was jammed with spectators. Near the end of the huge table at the front of the room, Senator Joseph R. McCarthy hunched over a microphone, reviling the Eisenhower administration. He claimed that high officials of the Eisenhower administration were arbitrarily silencing witnesses from the executive branch, and in doing so were preventing him from defending himself.

It was the eighteenth day of the already famous Army-McCarthy hearings, an exciting political drama that held the attention of an estimated 20 million television viewers. Over the weeks the Senator had sneered at Army Secretary Robert T. Stevens and anyone else who disagreed with him. His smirking disrespect and heavy-handed humor had already cooled the enthusiasm of many of his followers. Some had even turned against him. Senator McCarthy, in short, had created the worst possible climate in which to make any appeal to fair play or decency. And yet the Wisconsin Republican was now making such an appeal and would soon be receiving some sympathetic comment from Democratic as well as Republican senators.

The point at issue was simple: Should Army Counsel John Adams be required to testify as to conversations at a meeting at the Justice Department on January 21, 1954? Adams had already testified to being present on that day with Attorney

General Herbert Brownell, Jr., Deputy Attorney General William P. Rogers, Presidential Assistant Sherman Adams, White House Administrative Assistant Gerald D. Morgan, and United Nations Ambassador Henry Cabot Lodge. The meeting had been called to try to find ways to curb Senator McCarthy's free-wheeling investigation of the loyalty-security program in the Defense Department.

When, following this testimony on May 14, the Senate committee members asked for information about the conversations, Adams balked. He said that "instructions of the Executive Branch" barred him from telling of the conversations at that key meeting on January 21. Committee members were concerned. How could they obtain the evidence necessary to draw a conclusion on the hearings if they were to be barred from all "high-level discussions of the Executive Branch"?

The Army-McCarthy hearings centered on charges and countercharges involving Army Secretary Stevens, John G. Adams, Defense Department General Counsel H. Struve Hensel, Senator Joseph McCarthy, Roy M. Cohn, and Francis P. Carr. Cohn was chief counsel for McCarthy's Permanent Investigating Subcommittee, and Carr was chief investigator.

The Department of the Army alleged that Senator McCarthy, Cohn, and Carr had improperly used the power of the McCarthy subcommittee to obtain preferential treatment for Cohn's pal, Private G. David Schine. It was contended that the tough and aggressive little Cohn had tried to intimidate the Army and Defense officials to get Schine a commission or a special assignment as an assistant to the Secretary of the Army, or a post in the Central Intelligence Agency. It was also charged that Cohn had suggested that Private Schine might be given a special assignment to work with the McCarthy committee. In fact, Schine had been drafted and after a short time on regular Army duty was permitted to leave his regular duties to work with Cohn on the McCarthy committee investigations.

On the other side, Army Secretary Stevens contended that McCarthy and Cohn had launched a vindictive probe of the Army security programs in reprisal against those who had not co-operated to grant special treatment to Private Schine.

Senator McCarthy countercharged that the Army tried to blackmail his investigating subcommittee into dropping its investigation of the Army loyalty-security setup by threatening to circulate an embarrassing report about Cohn and Schine. The Wisconsin Senator declared that his investigation of the Army loyalty-security program was fully justified, and reiterated his charge that Major Irving Peress had been promoted by the Army despite his record as a "subversive." McCarthy did not deny that he had criticized Brigadier General Ralph Zwicker as a "disgrace" in uniform. And he renewed his assault on the Fort Monmouth Missile Research Center as a place honeycombed with "Reds."

It was easy to understand why the Eisenhower administration held the January 21 meeting at the Justice Department to decide how to handle Senator McCarthy. However, it was not so easy to understand why, after testifying there had been such a meeting, Army Counsel Adams refused to tell what was said.

Senator Stuart Symington, the handsome Missouri Democrat, was amazed that testimony would be barred on such a crucial meeting. He declared that testimony on the January 21 meeting was essential to determine the responsibility for the Defense Department's attempt to stop Senator Joseph McCarthy.

"This was a high-level discussion of the executive department, and this witness [Adams] has been instructed not to testify as to the interchange of views of people at that high-level meeting," explained Joseph N. Welch, the gentle-voiced

Boston lawyer who was serving as a special counsel for the Army.

"Does that mean we are going to get the information about low-level discussions but not about high-level discussions?" Senator Symington asked.

"That is only, sir, what I have been informed," Welch replied and then carefully made it clear he was not passing on the right or wrong of the policy. "It isn't a point of what I like. It is a point of what the witness has been instructed."

Senator Henry M. Jackson, the Washington Democrat, was no McCarthy supporter, but he too was nettled by the instructions given Adams by Deputy Defense Secretary Robert B. Anderson. Jackson held that if the Defense Department had any right to refuse to testify on high-level conversations, then it had waived that right when Adams told of the January 21 meeting and the participants.

"I think that maybe this testimony may be embarrassing to the Administration, and I do not think that because it is embarrassing to the Administration and favorable to Senator McCarthy, that it ought to be deleted," Senator Jackson declared.

"I think this committee should find out now," Jackson continued, "whether it [the Administration policy] covers just this conversation or whether it covers all conversations that went on between the various officials within the Executive Branch of Government . . . [if] we are going to be foreclosed here immediately from asking any further questions relating to conversations between officials within the Executive Branch. Heretofore, those conversations have been coming in when they have been favorable. Now that they are unfavorable [to the Administration], are they to be excluded?"

The unfairness of allowing favorable testimony by a witness, and then arbitrarily cutting off unfavorable testimony was apparent to many observers, even through the steam of feeling that surrounded the Army-McCarthy hearings. To justify such arbitrary secrecy, the Defense Department needed all the prestige it could summon.

The answer to the problem, it was decided, would be a letter from President Dwight D. Eisenhower to Defense Secretary Charles E. Wilson. It had to be a letter of high tone in which the popular President Eisenhower could convince the public that some great principle was at stake. It had to be general enough to avoid saying just why John Adams couldn't testify, but specific enough to give the impression that the security of the nation and the foundations of the Constitution were in danger if John Adams were forced to talk. The letter drafted between Friday, May 14, and Monday, May 17, carried the full impact of the prestige of a highly popular President, but it obscured temporarily a sweeping assumption of executive power to arbitrarily withhold information (see Appendix A).

On Monday morning, May 17, John Adams filed the Eisenhower letter with the Army-McCarthy committee and a broad new doctrine of "executive privilege" was born. The glowing phrases about a "proper separation of powers between the Executive and Legislative Branches of the Government," misled the public and a good many newspaper editorial writers and columnists, even though it did not fool all the members of the Army-McCarthy committee.

President Eisenhower's May 17, 1954, letter stated:

"Because it is essential to efficient and effective administration that employees of the Executive Branch be in a position to be completely candid in advising with each other on official matters, and because it is not in the public interest that any of their conversations or communications, or any documents or reproductions, concerning such advice be disclosed, you will instruct employees of your Department that in all of their appearances before the Subcommittee of the Senate Committee on Government Operations regarding the inquiry now before it they are not to testify to any such conversations or communications or to produce any such documents or reproductions. This principle must be maintained regardless of who would benefit by such disclosure.

"I direct this action so as to maintain the proper separation of powers between the Executive and Legislative Branches of the Government in accordance with my responsibilities under the Constitution. This separation is vital to preclude the exercise of arbitrary power by any branch of Government."

The Eisenhower letter also stated that "throughout our history the President has withheld information whenever he found that what was sought was confidential or its disclosure would be incompatible with the public interest or jeopardize the safety of the Nation." The letter gave the impression that from George Washington down, a number of Presidents had taken action analogous to the silencing of John Adams.

How was the "public interest or the safety of the Nation" to be jeopardized by Army Counsel John Adams' telling of a meeting on strategy to curb Senator McCarthy's investigations?

If this Eisenhower letter was "to preclude the exercise of arbitrary power by any branch of Government," then who was to stop the executive branch from such arbitrary silencing of witnesses?

Were the Army-McCarthy investigating committee and other committees of Congress to be barred from obtaining information on all "conversations or communications, or any documents or reproductions, concerning advice" within the executive branch?

These were the questions that immediately arose in the minds of Senator Jackson, Senator Symington, and Senator John L. McClellan, the Arkansas Democrat. Senator Everett Dirksen, the honey-voiced Illinois Republican, and Karl

Mundt, the South Dakota Republican who was serving as chairman, also expressed some concern, although privately.

Stern-faced Senator McClellan was not awed by the popularity of President Eisenhower or by the fact that Senator McCarthy was a highly unpopular figure at that point. He declared that if the barrier to any testimony on the January 21 meeting prevailed, then it would be impossible to establish whether John Adams, Army Secretary Stevens, or some higher officials were responsible for directing actions complained of by Senator McCarthy, Roy Cohn, and Private Schine.

"If the committee is going to be left in a dilemma of not knowing whether the Secretary [Stevens] is responsible for the action taken after that date [January 21], or whether the responsibility is at a higher level, then we will never be able to completely discharge our responsibility in this proceeding," Senator McClellan said.

Senator Jackson expressed the view that the secrecy policy left the committee "in a dilemma of passing on testimony that is incomplete. I think . . . that the Executive Branch is doing a great injustice to this committee and to all of the principals in this controversy by exercising the power which the President has, very late in the proceedings."

There was no question that President Eisenhower's letter had stalled the hearings at a crucial moment. If witnesses could not testify on an essential point, then there was little more that could be learned.

"I must admit that I am somewhat at a loss as to know what to do at the moment," Senator McCarthy said. "One of the subjects of this inquiry is to find out who was responsible for succeeding in calling off the hearing of Communist infiltration in Government. That the hearing was called off, no one can question."

McCarthy continued: "At this point, I find out there is no way of ever getting at the truth, because we do find that the charges were conceived, instigated, at a meeting [of January 21] which was testified to by Mr. Adams.

"I don't think the President is responsible for this," the Wisconsin Republican said in expressing his views that others had conceived the idea of silencing Adams and had merely obtained President Eisenhower's signature to accomplish their purpose. "I don't think his judgment is that bad.

"There is no reason why anyone should be afraid of the facts, of the truth, that came out of that meeting," Senator McCarthy thundered. "It is a very important meeting. It doesn't have to do with security matters. It doesn't have to do with national security. It merely has to do with why these charges were filed.

"The question is . . . how far can the President go? Who all can he order not to testify? If he can order the Ambassador to the U. N. [Henry Cabot Lodge] not to testify about something having nothing to do with the U. N., but a deliberate smear against my staff, then . . . any President can, by an executive order, keep the facts from the American people."

Senator McCarthy brought up the 1952 campaign in which government secrecy had been a key issue: "I do think that someone . . . should contact the President immediately and point out to him . . . that he and I and many of us campaigned and promised the American people that if they would remove our Democrat friends from control of the Government, then we would no longer engage in Government by secrecy, whitewash and cover-up."

It was a pathetic plea from a man who by now had completely destroyed his public image by his own brutal performance. His voice was raucous. His heavy beard gave him a rough, almost uncouth appearance despite his efforts to modify it by shaving during the noon recess.

Still, he hammered on. "I think that these facts should be

brought to the President because the American people will not stand for such as this, Mr. Chairman. They will not stand for a cover-up halfway through a hearing."

Seldom had there been more right on the side of McCarthy, but seldom had there been fewer people on his side. Many people who at first had been inclined to approve Joe McCarthy as "doing some good against the Communists," had been antagonized by his television image. Many editorial pages of a press that was normally much more objective had developed an attitude that anything that is bad for Joe McCarthy is good for the country.

Public sentiment against him was so strong that I did not believe it could have been changed to his favor—even if the committee had succeeded in eliciting testimony on the January 21, 1954, meeting and no matter how embarrassing it might have been to the Eisenhower administration.

There remained, nevertheless, the possibility that the Eisenhower letter could be used again. I was shocked at the wording of it. On the face of it, it seemed to extend the claim of "executive privilege" to prohibit Congress the access to *any* records or testimony that might involve communications within the executive branch. The letter was a directive with regard to excluding testimony in one hearing—the Army-McCarthy hearing. However, it was certainly broad enough that the Defense Department could use it to block any investigation.

Moreover, if an administration could successfully block any probe of high-level discussions in the Defense establishment, why couldn't it use that same "executive privilege" to block any investigation in any other executive agency? The thought disturbed me. The Teapot Dome scandals of the Harding administration could have been buried if those officials had applied even the mildest interpretation of "executive privilege" set down by President Eisenhower in the May 17 letter.

If cabinet officers and subordinate officials had refused to testify about the Teapot Dome affair on grounds of "confidential executive communications," it could have stifled the entire investigation by Senator Thomas Walsh, the Montana Democrat. Under the "executive privilege" theory, Secretary of Navy Edwin Denby and Secretary of Interior Albert B. Fall could have refused to give testimony or produce records of events leading up to the leasing of the Teapot Dome oil reserves. Fall's crimes might never have been uncovered, and he would have avoided the exposure and conviction.

Similarly, the tax scandals of the Truman administration could have been buried by claiming that all papers except those involving final decisions were "confidential executive communications." It had been vital to learn the nature of advice and recommendations of both high-level and low-level officials on settlements of huge tax cases. Attorney General J. Howard McGrath could have claimed that his conversations with T. Lamar Caudle, the Assistant Attorney General in charge of the Tax Division, were "confidential executive business."

Caudle and White House Aide Matthew Connelly could have claimed that their communications were "confidential executive business." As it was, the Caudle-Connelly communications were actually used as the basis of criminal charges on which Caudle and Connelly were convicted and sent to prison. A number of other officials of the Internal Revenue Service were convicted on charges arising out of revelation of the "advice and recommendations" they gave that were part of a huge tax "fix" operation.

I talked to several members of the Army-McCarthy committee, and with several of my newspaper colleagues, Democratic and Republican senators alike were disturbed at this seemingly limitless claim for "executive privilege." They hoped that the Eisenhower administration had written the letter for just this one hearing and had used the broad

language merely to avoid an impression that Senator Mc-
Carthy was being singled out for special treatment. Among
the newspaper reporters the attitude was that Joe McCarthy
was getting about what he had coming to him; there was
little concern over what use might be made of the precedent
in other investigations.

Many of the reporters had been misled by a memorandum
that accompanied the Eisenhower letter. It said, in effect,
that President Eisenhower was doing no more than George
Washington and many other Presidents had done. By invoking such names as George Washington and Thomas
Jefferson, the memorandum made it possible to pass off the
Eisenhower letter as a mere "clarification" of an old and settled principle. A close reading of "the precedents" disclosed
in fact that President Washington actually *opposed* withholding information from Congress. (See Chapter I.) He
once refused to deliver treaty papers to the House but only
because the Senate, not the House, had jurisdiction to ratify
treaties.

President Jefferson had taken papers into his personal
custody in connection with the Aaron Burr case, and thus
defied the federal court by declaring that the only way the
papers could be reached would be by impeaching him. He
was right. The law is quite settled on this point; neither the
courts nor the Congress can compel the President to testify
or produce personal letters, papers, and memorandums. President Jefferson eventually did send the documents subpoenaed by Chief Justice Marshall. But even if Jefferson had
refused to produce these documents, it would hardly seem
to be an adequate reason for allowing a lawyer for the Army
Department to refuse to testify about a meeting with a
cabinet officer and several White House aides.

The late Ed Milne, of the Washington Bureau of the
Providence *Journal*, shared my concern. He and I each wrote
stories demonstrating how the Truman tax scandals and the

Harding Teapot Dome scandals could have been hidden forever if "executive privilege" had barred testimony of all high-level conversations.

We also reminded our readers of the Republican reaction to the ducking and evasion of the Truman administration between 1946 and 1952. Senator Homer Ferguson, the Michigan Republican, was chairman of one of the committees that investigated the Truman administration in the late 1940s. His chief counsel at the time was William P. Rogers, who later became Eisenhower's Attorney General and a chief advocate of the ultimate in executive secrecy. Only a year before Eisenhower's election (September 27, 1951), Ferguson spoke out bluntly on the issue of suppression of facts by the executive departments: "It may be said that this practice of suppressing information in the executive department got its big start back in March, 1948. The Senator from Michigan [himself] was then chairman of the Senate Investigations Subcommittee and was investigating things that could be embarrassing to the administration. The subject of the investigation was the operation of the Government's loyalty program, revolving around the case of William Remington."

Senator Ferguson continued: "An executive order was issued, placing certain files under the direct and exclusive jurisdiction of the President. On occasion files were taken to the White House in order that they could not be subpoenaed. In the course of our hearings, an admiral was able to tell the Senator from Michigan, off the record, the fact that because of an order by the President of the United States he was not permitted to testify."

As I have shown (in Chapter III), the Truman administration did try to hide embarrassing facts from Congress. President Truman issued an executive order placing certain personnel files under a secrecy blanket, and on some occasions he ordered files delivered to his personal custody at the White House so they could not be reached by subpoena.

His administration stalled investigations of flagrant crimes for months. But President Truman never asserted any constitutional right by which all high-level officials could claim an "executive privilege" to refuse to testify or produce records.

The persistent, hard-hitting inquiries of Committee Counsel William P. Rogers made the Truman administration so frantic in 1948 and 1949 that a staff lawyer in the Justice Department was asked to prepare a memorandum on the precedents set by earlier Presidents who had withheld information from Congress. However, that memorandum was regarded as too insubstantial to use. The Truman administration relied instead on ducking and dodging to avoid embarrassment. It sensed correctly that the press and the public would have been outraged if it had tried to pull down a total secrecy curtain in the midst of investigations of the five percenters, the influence peddlers, and the loyalty cases.

What Truman would not do, however, the highly popular President Eisenhower did do. Ironically, his May 17 letter caused hardly a ripple of criticism. On the contrary, most editorial pages praised President Eisenhower for expressing some fine new theory on the U. S. Constitution or wrote off the letter as an historically unimportant, one-shot claim of secrecy.

I called one editor friend the day after such an approving editorial appeared, and commented that the Eisenhower doctrine of "executive privilege" could bar Congress from practically any executive papers containing "opinions, advice or recommendations."

"This will set the 'Freedom of Information' cause back fifty years, if it is not criticized and stopped now," I said.

My editor friend said he thought that there might have been some loyalty file discussed at the January 21 meeting, and that this would be a justification for refusing testimony.

I told him that no one had claimed that loyalty files were discussed, and that if this had been the reason for the secrecy then it should have been stated. Also, I pointed out that while discussion of a loyalty file might give some justifications for limiting testimony, the limitation should only cover that subject and not the whole meeting.

The editor agreed with me that the broad language of the Eisenhower letter constituted a dangerous precedent. But he didn't believe that any administration would ever try to invoke the total arbitrary "executive privilege."

Just how wrong events would prove him to be was not then easy to predict. Indeed, the whole story of the Army-McCarthy hearings had by this time taken second news billing to the United States Supreme Court ruling on school segregation. The unanimous segregation decision came out on May 17, 1954—the same date as the Eisenhower letter to Wilson. That segregation decision now dominated discussions of constitutional law. And the few persons who did stop to think about the inherent threat in the broad use of secrecy could hardly get emotional about it—as long as the only victims appeared to be Senator McCarthy and his little knot of followers.

CHAPTER V

Another Blow at Senator Joe

When the Eisenhower administration took office in January 1953, I had had high hopes that arbitrary government secrecy would be ended. As a candidate, the President had talked much of his interest in open government and had pledged to make all but national security information available to the public. So had the Vice President, Richard M. Nixon.

As late as November 6, 1953, Attorney General Herbert Brownell, Jr., was continuing to stress the Republican party's interest in eliminating secrecy policies of the Truman administration. In Chicago, before a convention of Associated Press Managing Editors, Brownell said he was "very much aware of the great importance of seeing to it that the obstacles to the free flow of information are kept to an absolute minimum.

"I would like to call attention to some of the procedures which we established," Brownell said. "At the very outset of the new Administration, we provided that any pardons or commutations of sentence shall be a matter of public record. Throughout the prior Administration, these executive actions were taken secretly, for political purposes and over the objection of the Office of the Pardon Attorney.

"We also started the policy of making a matter of public record matters which our predecessors buried in secrecy, such as settlements of all types of cases which we handle and involve monetary considerations, such as tax claims, damage suits and Alien Property settlements. We do not contend that we have achieved perfection in our efforts to provide a full flow of information. But we are working on it and each day find new ways to do our part."

At this same meeting, Attorney General Brownell announced that President Eisenhower was revoking a much criticized executive order by President Truman dealing with defense information. He said President Eisenhower was issuing a new order which "attains the required balance between the need to protect certain types of defense information, and the need for keeping the citizens of a republic as fully informed as possible concerning what their government is doing.

"President Eisenhower considers the free flow of information from the Government to the people to be basic to the good health of the Nation," Brownell told the editors. He declared that under the Truman administration there "was a tendency to follow the dangerous policy heretofore used by dictator nations of authorizing government officials to use the term 'National Security' indiscriminately, and thereby throw a veil of secrecy over many items which historically have been open to the public in this country."

The Attorney General said he viewed the new Republican policy as an opportunity to "demonstrate to all the world the vivid contrast between our system of government, which believes in and practices freedom of the press, and the Communist system, which regards the concept of freedom of information as a threat to the continuance of its tyrannical rule."

Such attitudes in November 1953 were difficult to reconcile with those of May 1954, when the same Attorney General was helping fashion a policy that was more devastating to a free flow of information than simply refusing to give information to the press. The May 17, 1954, letter from

President Eisenhower to the Defense Department said in essence that any high officials of the Defense establishment might refuse to produce records or testify even when suppoenaed by a properly constituted congressional committee that was acting within its jurisdiction.

The Army-McCarthy hearings that had given rise to the famous letter ended on June 17, 1954. However, it was not necessary to wait for the official reports made public on October 30, 1954, to know that Senator McCarthy was finished as a political power—and that the administration would use the "executive privilege" precedent again.

As an aftermath of the Army-McCarthy hearings, a charge was filed that Senator McCarthy had conducted himself in a manner "unbecoming a member of the United States Senate." And on August 2, 1954, the U. S. Senate decided by the overwhelming vote of 75 to 12 to investigate Senator McCarthy's conduct.

Senator Arthur V. Watkins, a Utah Republican, was named chairman of the select McCarthy Censure Committee to determine recommendations on Senator McCarthy's conduct. In barely more than a month Chairman Watkins ran smack into a roadblock of "executive privilege."

The subject of inquiry was Senator McCarthy's severe tongue lashing of Brigadier General Ralph Zwicker, of Camp Kilmer, N. J. Major General Kirke B. Lawton, a former commanding general of Fort Monmouth, N. J., refused to testify about conversations with General Zwicker. He claimed "executive privilege" under the May 17, 1954, letter from President Eisenhower.

Edward Bennett Williams, who was serving as counsel for Senator McCarthy, questioned the applicability of the May 17 letter: "Don't you know, General, that order of May 17, 1954, referred only to the Government Operations Committee and the hearing then in session which was commonly known as the Army-McCarthy hearing?"

General Lawton replied that he had been advised that the May 17 letter "not only applied to the so-called Mundt committee [the Special Committee for the Army-McCarthy hearings] but it applies to this or any other."

Chairman Watkins excused General Lawton and wrote Defense Secretary Charles E. Wilson asking clarification. Defense Secretary Wilson replied that Generals Lawton and Zwicker would be allowed to testify and produce documents unless their action would be "in violation of national security regulations or a violation of the President's order of May 17, 1954."

There could be little doubt now that the Defense Department intended to make the May 17, 1954, letter a part of its basic doctrine with all of the great blanket of secrecy that this would provide. I was now more concerned than ever, for I had hoped that the May 17 letter was the one-shot secrecy claim that so many of my colleagues thought it was. But again the name of Joe McCarthy was mixed up in the investigation, and in 1954 it would have been difficult to get any cool thinking on a subject that remotely touched on the controversial Wisconsin Republican.

Still, I couldn't help worrying that the new and expanded doctrine of "executive privilege" was just too convenient a cover for those who wished to hide their activities from Congress, the press, or the public. It could be used by the incompetent as well as the corrupt.

This doctrine of an "inherent right" of persons in the executive departments to refuse testimony or documents threatened our whole system of government. It seemed a naked claim of an authority for unlimited secrecy, without regard for laws or the spirit of a democracy. By claiming a right to withhold all information on opinions, conclusions, recommendations, or suggestions, this doctrine could allow the secrecy blanket to be dropped over virtually every document in most agencies, for there are few governmental documents that do not contain some opinions or suggestions. It carried within it, in short, the seeds of dictatorship.

It seemed strange to me that this doctrine would be set forth in the administration of a President who would be regarded as one of the mildest Chief Executives, and certainly one of the least inclined toward dictatorial action. I was not worried that President Eisenhower would try to use it as a tool for totalitarianism. But with this doctrine in force a man who was inclined toward totalitarian methods might readily administer the laws as he pleased.

CHAPTER VI

Secrecy Fix on Dixon and Yates

Not until the summer of 1955 did it become apparent that the May 17, 1954, Eisenhower letter would be used on matters unrelated to Senator Joseph R. McCarthy. Throughout the fall and winter of 1954, I spoke and wrote about the potential danger of "executive privilege" as it had been applied in the Army-McCarthy hearings and in the McCarthy censure hearings. A few persons saw it my way. But the general tendency to believe that the letter was written solely to deal with Senator McCarthy held fast, and a general faith prevailed that the Eisenhower administration would not use it to cover up mistakes, corruption, or improprieties.

Then suddenly, in June 1955, the White House reinvoked the letter as justification for refusing to make records available to a Senate committee investigating the Dixon-Yates contract.

First, Budget Director Rowland R. Hughes used "executive privilege" to conceal testimony and documents requested by Senator Estes Kefauver, the Tennessee Democrat in charge of the investigation.

Then J. Sinclair Armstrong, the chairman of the Securities and Exchange Commission, used "executive privilege" to justify his refusal to disclose conversations with Presidential Assistant Sherman Adams relative to postponing a hearing on Dixon-Yates financing.

Also, Sherman Adams claimed the "privilege" not to be

required to testify about his talks with Armstrong or about other activity in the Dixon-Yates contract development.

At last a few of the Democrats who had been only too glad to see "executive privilege" invoked against Senator McCarthy opened their eyes. The realization of the danger dawned too late, however, for it would take more than a few weeks to upset a precedent that only a year earlier had been generally viewed as praiseworthy.

While the Army-McCarthy hearings and the McCarthy censure affair dominated the news, top-level officials in the Eisenhower administration had been quietly at work arranging for the Mississippi Valley Generating Company to furnish 600,000 kilowatts of electricity to the Tennessee Valley Authority. The Mississippi Valley Generating Company contract ultimately became known as the "Dixon-Yates" contract because of the two men responsible for its creation. They were Edgar H. Dixon, president of Middle South Utilities, Inc., and Eugene A. Yates, chairman of the board of The Southern Company. Both firms act as holding companies for utilities operating in Arkansas, Georgia, Louisiana, Mississippi, and Alabama. Dixon and Yates joined forces to create the Mississippi Valley Generating Company, an operating subsidiary in West Memphis, Ark. The Dixon-Yates contract was reported to be for the purpose of replacing power in the Tennessee Valley Authority area that was used by the Atomic Energy Commission.

Lewis L. Strauss, then chairman of the Atomic Energy Commission (AEC), and Joseph Dodge, then Director of the Budget, were active in pushing this contract. Chairman Strauss pushed it despite the fact that a majority of the Atomic Energy Commissioners were opposed to such a contract on grounds there was no Atomic Energy Commission installation near West Memphis, Ark., and the power was to be used in Memphis, Tenn.

The Eisenhower administration had opposed the Tennes-

see Valley Authority proposal to build a steam plant at
Fulton, Tenn., with a capacity of 500,000 kilowatts to provide for the power needs of Memphis, plus a surplus for
industrial expansion. Budget Director Dodge opposed the
Fulton steam plant and axed the 90 million dollars requested
from the budget in 1953. Gordon Clapp, at that time chairman of the TVA, then asked that to offset the loss of the
Fulton steam plant the AEC consumption of TVA power be
cut sharply. It was at this point that Budget Director Dodge
turned to the AEC in an effort to get that agency to find ways
to obtain power from a private company.

The Dixon-Yates contract idea developed over a period of
months in 1953 and early 1954. Dozens of conferences were
held in which one of the important figures was Adolphe
Wenzell, a vice president and director of the First Boston
Corporation. Wenzell was an engineer and an expert in the
cost of construction of public utility plants. From May 20,
1953, to September 3, 1953, he made studies and issued reports on TVA power plant costs. In January 1954, Rowland
R. Hughes, then Deputy Director of the Budget, asked Wenzell to assist the Budget Bureau on the Dixon-Yates contract.
Wenzell agreed and, until April 10, 1954, continued to par-
ticipate in the Dixon-Yates negotiations.

Wenzell continued to draw his salary from First Boston
Corporation, and received travel costs and a per diem allow-
ance from the government for his services for the Budget
Bureau. Since First Boston Corporation was slated to be un-
derwriter of the Mississippi Valley Generating Company, a
question was raised by his associates about the propriety of
Wenzell's services to the Budget Bureau and to First Boston
—a firm that had a pecuniary interest in the Dixon-Yates
contract agreement.

As the Dixon-Yates contract moved toward completion, a
lawyer for the law firm of Sullivan & Cromwell told Wenzell
that before First Boston should take part in the financing

for Dixon-Yates, Wenzell "should make clear that he had severed his entire relations with the Bureau of the Budget."

In the summer of 1954, a few complaints were raised about the Dixon-Yates contract. There was also opposition to the Dixon-Yates contract within the Tennessee Valley Authority as well as by a majority of the Atomic Energy Commissioners. But on June 16, 1954, Rowland Hughes, by then promoted to Director of the Budget, wrote to the Atomic Energy Commission:

"The President has asked me to instruct the Atomic Energy Commission to proceed with negotiations with the sponsors of the proposal made by Messrs. Dixon and Yates with a view of signing a definite contract."

The contract was signed, and in the following weeks the number of Democratic complaints mounted. The complaints hit a number of points. The Democrats contended that the Dixon-Yates contract could cost the government from 107 million to 120 million dollars over a period of twenty-five years, but that in the end the government wouldn't own the plant. This was compared to the 90 million cost for the Fulton steam plant which the TVA wanted to construct.

The debate revolved largely around the question of private versus public power (or TVA). Many Democrats held that the Eisenhower administration was allowing the public treasury to be milked by Big Business in the same fashion the Harding administration had permitted the exploitation of Navy oil reserves in the Teapot Dome scandals.

Democratic National Chairman Stephen Mitchell hit a sensitive nerve in early August 1954 when he implied that President Eisenhower had direct responsibility for the Dixon-Yates contract. He charged that one of President Eisenhower's golfing associates was a director of The Southern Company, one of the two holding companies that had established the Mississippi Valley Generating Company. Mitchell's office identified the man as Bobby Jones, former

amateur and professional golfing champion. No evidence
was ever produced to support the insinuation that Jones
influenced Dixon-Yates decisions.

President Eisenhower was furious that his associations
would be subject to such charges, and in his August 17, 1954,
press conference he offered to disclose all the events leading
up to the Dixon-Yates contract.

"Any one of you here present might singly or in an investigation group go to the Bureau of the Budget, or to the
Chief of the Atomic Energy Commission, and get the complete record from the inception of the idea [of the Dixon-
Yates contract] to this very minute, and it is all yours."

Four days later, on August 21, 1954, the Atomic Energy
Commission released what was purported to be a full chronology of all events in the development of the Dixon-Yates
contract. The names of Wenzell and Paul Miller, assistant
vice president of First Boston Corporation, had appeared in
an original draft. However, the names of both of these First
Boston Corporation officials—Wenzell and Miller—were eliminated from the chronology that was given to the press.

On the surface, it appeared that President Eisenhower had
met charges of improper activity with a frank and open
report on the whole record of the Dixon-Yates contract. Not
until February 18, 1955, did anyone charge that the chronology was not a full truthful report. On that day, Senator
Lister Hill, the Alabama Democrat, made a Senate speech
in which he charged Wenzell with a dual role in the Dixon-
Yates negotiations. He questioned the propriety of Wenzell's
being a financial adviser to Dixon-Yates while at the same
time serving as an adviser to the United States Government
on the Dixon-Yates contract.

Spokesmen for the Eisenhower administration such as
Budget Director Rowland R. Hughes denied there was any
dual role by Wenzell in the Dixon-Yates contract. As late as
June 27, 1955, Budget Director Hughes testified before a

Senate committee that "I was told it was not true." He said he didn't know that First Boston had anything to do with the financing of Dixon-Yates.

The speech by Senator Hill caused understandable concern in the White House and among the top officials of the First Boston Corporation. Revelation of a "conflict of interest" could spoil the entire 107-million-dollar contract and its profits for First Boston. It could undo what President Eisenhower and many top subordinates deemed an important block to the spread of the Tennessee Valley Authority.

Of immediate importance was a 6.5-million-dollar appropriation slated to go to the House of Representatives on June 13, 1955. The appropriation was for a transmission line from the Tennessee Valley Authority to the point where it would pick up power from the Mississippi Valley Generating Company in the middle of the Mississippi River.

On June 11, 1955, Sherman Adams telephoned to J. Sinclair Armstrong, chairman of the Securities Exchange Commission. He requested that the SEC hold up hearings on debt financing of the Dixon-Yates contract until after the House had finished work on the 6.5-million-dollar appropriation. Wenzell was among the witnesses scheduled to testify before the SEC, and testimony on Wenzell's full role in Dixon-Yates could have had a devastating impact on the appropriation. The hearings were postponed.

Finally, on June 28, 1955, Budget Director Hughes revealed that the Eisenhower administration was going to try to pull down the secrecy curtain on the investigation of Dixon-Yates. The claim of "executive privilege" was to be the vehicle.

Hughes was being questioned by Senator Estes Kefauver, regarding a request for the opportunity to examine all memoranda, documents, and reports pertinent to the Dixon-Yates contract. By this time it was abundantly clear to the Kefauver subcommittee that the chronology released on August 21, 1954, was intentionally incomplete.

Indirectly Hughes moved to "executive privilege."

"As pointed out to you," he told Senator Kefauver, "we operate under the President's general instructions with regard to interoffice and intraoffice staff material, that such material is not to be made public.

"All documents which involve final decisions of public policy have of course already been made public," Hughes said in an effort to give the impression that the administration had complied with the President's pledge of frankness. "You [Kefauver] pointed out that you interpreted the President's statement at a press conference last fall to indicate that they [the "executive privilege" claims] did not apply to this case. I have checked on this matter and I am authorized by the President to state that his general instructions stand but that we, of course, stand on the decision to make every pertinent paper or document that can be made public under this ruling available to you."

Hughes was trying to give an impression of frankness, while at the same time reserving to the administration the right to withhold any Dixon-Yates information they wished to regard as "interoffice and intraoffice staff material." Hughes continued:

"A quick review of our files last night disclosed no other papers or documents to be added to the somewhat voluminous releases already made, but we shall make a full and careful search in the next few days to confirm this or to pick out material, if any, which should be added to that previously released."

Hughes had left the Eisenhower administration an "out" on any omissions of material. Next he sought to absolve Wenzell from any connection with the Dixon-Yates contract.

"We have also reviewed the report which Mr. Wenzell made as an adviser in September, 1953, and find that that had nothing to do with the Dixon-Yates contract and, as a confidential document under the general ruling [of "executive privilege"], therefore cannot be made available to your committee."

Although Hughes concluded with a promise to "cooperate where we can do so properly," he made it clear the Eisenhower administration was still going to use the "executive privilege" claim to secrecy if it wanted to refuse testimony or records.

Up to this time, high administration officials had deleted information, twisted the record, engaged in half truths and full deception to obscure the story of the Dixon-Yates contract. Now they were seeking to use the name of President Eisenhower, and give the impression that some constitutional principle was involved in hiding the records.

Senator Kefauver took to the Senate floor to lash out at the concealment of records and testimony in the Dixon-Yates investigation. At the presidential press conference on June 30, 1955, Frank Van De Linden, of the Nashville *Banner*, forced the issue with President Eisenhower:

"Senator Kefauver charged on the Senate floor yesterday that the Budget Bureau was trying to conceal what he called a scandal in the Dixon-Yates contract negotiation regarding the employment of Mr. Adolphe Wenzell, of the First Boston Corporation," Van De Linden said. "Senator Knowland says there is no corruption in it, and that he thinks you were just trying to help the Tennessee Valley get some power. I wonder if Mr. Hughes, of the Budget Bureau, had cleared with you his refusal to give Mr. Kefauver the information he was asking down there?"

President Eisenhower answered: "Mr. Hughes came to see me, went over the situation, and I repeated the general instructions—I think that I expressed some in front of this body —that every single pertinent paper in the Yates-Dixon contract, from its inception until the final writing of the contract, would be made available, I think I said, at that time to the press, much less to any committee."

After seeming to approve an open record, he then quali-fied it: "Now, I do stand on this: Nobody has a right to go in and just . . . wrecking the processes of Government by tak-ing every single file—and some of you have seen our file rooms and know their size—and wrecking the entire filing system and paralyzing the processes of Government while they are going through them."

The President rambled on: "There are—these files are filled with every kind of personal note—I guess my own files are filled with personal notes from my own staff all through; they are honeycombed with them. Well, now, to drag those things out where a man says to me, 'I think so-and-so is a bad per-son to appoint, to so-and-so, and you shouldn't have him,' all he had was his own opinion. You can't drag those things out and put them before the public with justice to anybody, and we are not going to do it."

President Eisenhower had engaged in a lot of conversation unrelated to the information sought. Now he indicated that he personally believed that officials of his administration had already put out all pertinent documents:

"At the time that I gave those instructions, Mr. Hughes and Mr. Strauss, whoever else was involved, got together ev-ery single document that was pertinent to this thing and put it out."

The President concluded with a complete approval of the Wenzell role: "Now, as far as the Wenzell report, Mr. Wen-zell was never called in or asked a single thing about the Yates-Dixon contract. He was brought into—as a technical adviser in the very early days when none of us here knew about the bookkeeping methods of the TVA or anything else. He was brought in as a technical adviser and nothing else and before this contract was ever even proposed."

President Eisenhower seemed to have no information

about Wenzell's role after January 1954. His comments seemed completely contrary to the testimony already taken before the Kefauver Subcommittee on Antitrust and Monopoly. I followed up the Van De Linden question.

"Mr. President," I said. "A little while ago you stated that Mr. Wenzell was never called in about the Yates-Dixon contract, and there seemed to be some testimony before the SEC and before a committee that he served as a consultant. I wonder if you were—"

The President cut in to answer that "He [Wenzell] did serve as a consultant at one time."

"Of Dixon-Yates?" I asked it fast.

"No; I think—now, I will check this up," the President started. "My understanding is that quickly as the Dixon-Yates thing came up he resigned, and we got as our consultant a man named Adams from the Power Commission here itself to come over and be consultant so as to have him because he [Wenzell] was connected with a great Boston financial company."

"Mr. President," I asked. "Had you been informed that he had no connection at all with the Dixon-Yates—?"

"My understanding of it, and it may have been—that part of it there may have been—an overlap of a week or two, there I am not sure of," President Eisenhower answered. It was difficult to understand he had so little information on the key issue at this late date.

"Would there be any change in your position on that if there was material that he [Wenzell] had served as a consultant on that [Dixon-Yates]?" I asked.

"If he had served as a consultant on that [Dixon-Yates] and brought in a definite recommendation to us I would be very delighted to make that public," President Eisenhower answered. "But I just don't believe there is a thing in it about it. However, I will have it checked again."

Noting the press conference statement, Senator Kefauver fired off a quick letter to President Eisenhower:

"My Dear Mr. President: I have just been informed that in answer to questions of the press today you are recorded as saying that Mr. Adolphe H. Wenzell was never called in or asked a single thing about the Dixon-Yates contract, and that as quickly as the Dixon-Yates matter came up Mr. Wenzell resigned. However, you say you will have it checked again."

Then Senator Kefauver followed up with a careful chronological study of the testimony of Wenzell and other key officials in the Eisenhower administration which showed that Wenzell had been a consultant on the Dixon-Yates contract. It also showed that high Eisenhower administration officials knew, or should have known, the precise role that Wenzell had filled.

At his next press conference, on July 6, 1955, President Eisenhower said Wenzell's role was perfectly "proper" in Dixon-Yates, but indicated there was a chance the contract might be canceled.

Senator Kefauver sought an explanation of the Sherman Adams calls to the SEC that had postponed hearings on the financial arrangements for Dixon-Yates at the crucial point before the House took up the appropriation measure.

On July 21, Adams refused to testify before the Kefauver investigating subcommittee. In a letter to Senator Kefauver he stated that he could not give testimony because of his confidential relationship to the President, and also because "every fact as to which I might give testimony either has been or could be testified to fully by other responsible government officials."

The same day Kenneth Fields, general manager of the Atomic Energy Commission, wrote to Kefauver declining to furnish documents on ground they were "privileged communications within the executive branch." Earlier, SEC

Chairman Armstrong had made his first refusal to testify on his conversations with Sherman Adams.

Senator Kefauver replied to Adams that there had been consistent claims of "executive privilege" that barred the investigators from obtaining the truth.

"No official of the Government," the Senator wrote, "no matter how high his position can properly claim privilege when a committee of Congress is seeking the facts in respect to corruption."

Senator Kefauver stated: "In these circumstances a claim of privilege is tantamount to suppression of evidence of possible crime and corruption. Not even the privilege of attorney-client can be used for such a nefarious purpose."

Sherman Adams hid out behind the protective walls of the White House, unavailable for questioning by Congress and unavailable for questioning by the press. "Executive privilege," as smoothly practiced by the Eisenhower administration, made it appear that Adams was invulnerable to attack, or even questioning, on any of his activities. Perhaps he *was* the cold and clean New Hampshire granite of the legend of Sherman Adams. Perhaps he *was* the dispassionate, efficient barrier against the corrupting influences of personal and political favoritism. But, even if Sherman Adams were the puritanic guardian of good government as pictured, the idea of surrounding any man's activities with such arbitrary secrecy was a bad principle. It was an open invitation to misuse of power and influence that few could withstand.

At the July 27, 1955, press conference I questioned President Eisenhower to determine what he knew of the activities of Sherman Adams in the Dixon-Yates affair.

"Mr. President," I said. "There has been testimony of the SEC Chairman [J. Sinclair Armstrong] that Sherman Adams intervened before the SEC, which was a quasi-judicial body. Testimony was given by the chairman on that score.

"The Democrats are contending that there was something

improper in intervening with any quasi-judicial body. I wonder if you looked into that and if you have any comment you would like to make about it."

The President replied that he had "looked into it only to this extent: I am sure that Mr.—head of the commission—has given the entire story. I understand that he is back before the committee. And certainly if he has omitted any details, he should give them now."

The President continued: "And I believe that Governor Adams has informed the Senate committee that he hasn't a single detail to add; that the story has been told and that is all there is to it."

Garnett Horner, the White House reporter for the Washington *Star*, came in with another question:

"In connection with the Dixon-Yates matter, and in view of the fact that the Senate investigation subcommittee recently brought out the first time the part played in initiating the Dixon-Yates contract by Adolphe Wenzell, of the First Boston Corporation, which corporation later became the financing agent for Dixon-Yates. In view of all that, do you believe your directions last summer for disclosure of the complete record in the case were carried out by the agencies [the Bureau of the Budget and the Atomic Energy Commission] concerned?"

President Eisenhower replied: "Well, I didn't know that anyone had alleged that he [Wenzell] was the initiator, because no such statement has ever been made to me.

"But what I have done is this: I have gotten back Mr. Dodge, who was Director of the Budget when all this was done, when the 1954, I believe, policy on this statement, on this whole proposition was made, and he is going now before one of the committees."

The President turned to Press Secretary James C. Hagerty to ask: "Isn't that correct?"

Hagerty answered, "Yes, sir."

The President continued: "He [Dodge] is going down before one of the committees with instruction to do this: to tell every possible item that has anything whatsoever to bear on Dixon-Yates, and see whether we can get the whole list of information properly coordinated and placed before the people that are investigating it."

President Eisenhower still had not answered the question relative to whether he knew that his August 1954 order on complete disclosure on Dixon-Yates had been violated. I followed up the question of Garnett Horner:

"I hate to go back to Dixon-Yates again, but there was one thing I don't think was completely clear. There were some AEC officials, Mr. Fields and Mr. Cook, who testified that Mr. Wenzell's name was knowingly eliminated from the Dixon-Yates chronology; and, of course, they stated this was on the recommendations of the Bureau of the Budget.

"I wonder if you knew anything of this, and if you did know of it, if you would like to comment on whether you thought it was important."

[On July 21, 1955, Kenneth E. Fields, general manager, Atomic Energy Commission, and Richard W. Cook, deputy general manager, Atomic Energy Commission, testified before the Senate Judiciary subcommittee. Fields identified Cook as the man who prepared the chronology.

"The Bureau of the Budget suggested that we leave them (the names of Wenzell and Miller) out," Cook said in answer to a question from Senator Joseph O'Mahoney.

"I can assure you that we did not try to conceal anything," Cook continued. "They just called to our attention certain minor entries that . . . didn't appear to be appropriate."

"So they suggested no other names that you leave out except Wenzell and Miller?" Senator Kefauver asked.

"No; not that I recall," Cook answered.]

The President knew little about the Dixon-Yates contract even at this late date, more than a year after it had first been criticized by Democrats. His answer reflected his lack of knowledge, as well as his desire to shut off further questions.

"I don't intend to comment on it any more at all," he said. "Now, I think I have given to this conference time and again, the basic elements of this whole development, and everything I could possibly be expected to know about it.

"I said Mr. Dodge, who initiated this whole thing, is going down before the committee to again begin the process of taking this thing from its inception and following it through until he turned [it] over to Mr. Hughes, and I believe that Mr. Hughes is to be there if they want him again.

"Now, they [Dodge and Hughes] can tell the entire story, and I don't know exactly such details as that. How could I be expected to know? I never heard of it."

It would have been difficult to imagine a case that dramatized more clearly the bad government that could fester under arbitrary executive secrecy. President Eisenhower had issued an order for a full chronology of events leading up to the Dixon-Yates contract, but, instead, his subordinates had put out a record edited to eliminate the names of persons involved in a "conflict of interest."

The secrecy deceived the public, deceived the committee of Congress, and even deceived President Eisenhower. His comments over the period of months showed that his subordinates had misled or deliberately deceived him on the key point in the controversy—the role of Adolphe Wenzell. In this respect the secrecy possible under "executive privilege" worked against the best interests of President Eisenhower. Apparently his subordinates thought they could distort the record, and keep it hidden from the public and the President. Only the persistent work of Senator Kefauver's investigators pulled loose sufficient facts to document the deception.

President Eisenhower might have been able to sell the Dixon-Yates contract to the public if it had been handled as a simple debate of private power versus public power. But he could no longer see it through once he had been forced to take note of a "conflict of interest" that he had previously denied existed.

Cancellation of the Dixon-Yates contract did not end the Eisenhower administration's problem with that ill-fated venture. It was to be a major factor in 1959 in blocking the nomination of Lewis L. Strauss as Secretary of Commerce.

In November of 1955, William Mitchell, counsel for the Atomic Energy Commission, made a report stating: "It appears that Wenzell, while having a conflicting private interest, acted as one of the principal advisers of the government" in the negotiating of the Dixon-Yates contract. Mitchell called attention to the many meetings in which Wenzell had taken part as a government official in the first four months of 1954.

"The matters on which Wenzell was advising the contractor [Dixon-Yates] were the same on which he had been employed to advise the government," Mitchell stated officially for the AEC.

When the government canceled the contract on grounds of a "conflict of interest," the Dixon-Yates group claimed that tremendous expenditures had already been made on the contract. When Dixon and Yates sued the government for $3,-534,788, the Justice Department was forced to go to court with legal briefs and facts to support the government contention that Wenzell's role was a "conflict of interests."

Thus Attorney General Brownell's department was in court to give evidence of an impropriety that President Eisenhower had said did not exist.

Less than a year later, on August 11, 1956, Senator Estes Kefauver and Senator Joseph O'Mahoney, the Wyoming Democrat, insisted on action against those engaged in concealing the facts.

Senator Kefauver charged that Sherman Adams and other "high officials of the Eisenhower administration" violated the criminal law in their handling of the Dixon-Yates contract. He named the other high officials as Lewis L. Strauss, chairman of the Atomic Energy Commission and the President's adviser on atomic energy matters; Rowland R. Hughes, former Director of the Budget; and J. Sinclair Armstrong, chairman of the SEC.

In asking Attorney General Herbert Brownell to present the matter to a federal grand jury, Kefauver commented:

"Indictments and convictions have been obtained under Section 371 of Title 18 of the United States Code in cases involving similar circumstances. The offense under this section of the Criminal Code is that of conspiring to defraud the United States Government. The essential ingredient of the offense under this section of the Criminal Code is the failure of a government official to discharge conscientiously the duties of his office and administer Federal law in an unbiased manner."

Kefauver continued: "In this case there exists substantial evidence indicating that Mr. Adams, Mr. Hughes and Mr. Strauss deliberately attempted to conceal the conflict of interest growing out of Mr. Wenzell's dual role in the Dixon-Yates deal—a conflict which the President's own Attorney General now labels so contrary to public policy as to render the agreement null and void."

Senator O'Mahoney characterized the Dixon-Yates matter as violating "every concept of decent government and fair and impartial administration of applicable law."

The stentorian-toned Wyoming Senator gave a "partial listing of the wreckage left strewn in the path" of Dixon-Yates!

1. "The independent character of the Atomic Energy Commission and the Tennessee Valley Authority was brought into serious question.

2. "Officials of the Department of Justice and the Securities and Exchange Commission were placed in the position

of having been persuaded to take legal positions which ran counter to precedent of many years standing.

3. "The administration of the law by SEC was brought into disrepute because of SEC's flagrant departures from accepted interpretations of the Public Utility Holding Company Act and its succumbing to pressures from 'higher authority' emanating from the White House.

4. "AEC was forced to execute and sponsor a contract which the Department of Justice has since asserted violated the Holding Company Act, the Atomic Energy Act, and the conflict of interest statutes."

O'Mahoney said that there "is no way that we can ascertain the full facts" because "the Subcommittee has been completely blocked from getting to the bottom of the Dixon-Yates contract by the very men in the White House who were involved in these negotiations."

After this debacle, it surprised me more than ever to discover that few people saw the full evil of the broad principle of "executive privilege" as set out in the May 17, 1954, letter.

There was still a general lack of awareness of the possible dictatorial power lurking behind the secrecy curtain.

As I have said, I did not believe that President Eisenhower would knowingly use secrecy to cover crimes, but I had doubts about some people in his administration. Even if it could be assumed that every member of his administration was totally honest, "executive privilege" was still too potentially dangerous a doctrine to have in force.

It was not until January 9, 1961, that the Supreme Court of the United States stated the final words on the Dixon-Yates contract. Chief Justice Warren delivered the opinion of the Court that Adolphe H. Wenzell had been involved in a "conflict of interest" which was a violation of the law (18 U.S.C. 434).

The law states: "Whoever, being an officer, agent or member of, or directly or indirectly interested in the pecuniary

profits or contracts of any corporation . . . is employed or
acts as an officer or agent of the United States for the transaction of business with such business entity, shall be fined
not more than $2,000 or imprisoned not more than two years,
or both."

No criminal charge was brought against Wenzell, but the
majority opinion stated that the civil law suit by the Dixon-
Yates group involved "fundamental questions relating to the
standards of conduct which should govern those who represent the Government in its business dealings.

"The question is whether the Government may disaffirm
a contract which is infected by an illegal contract," the majority opinion stated. "As we have indicated, the public policy embodied in Section 434 requires nonenforcement [of the
Dixon-Yates contract] and this is true even though the conflict of interest was caused or condoned by high government
officials."

The Eisenhower administration, as I have already stated,
could probably have made a winning argument for the
Dixon-Yates contract in a debate involving simply public
power versus private power. However, the temptation to use
the secrecy of "executive privilege" proved too great, and
ironically the secrecy kept President Eisenhower in the dark
about the details of the role of Adolphe H. Wenzell until it
was too late. Excessive secrecy blinded President Eisenhower
and some of his assistants until they were so victimized by
deceit that they could not recover their equilibrium and
salvage the Dixon-Yates contract.

CHAPTER VII

Congress Becomes Concerned

In late 1954 and early 1955, secrecy obscured the facts in a major controversy over administration of the government loyalty-security program. The Republicans had campaigned in 1952 on a charge that the Truman administration was "soft" on Communists and contended that an administration headed by Adlai Stevenson could be expected to be composed of many Communist "coddlers." In the 1954 congressional election campaigns the Republicans used statistics compiled by the Eisenhower administration to continue to assert that Democrats were "soft" on Communists.

The Democrats contended that the Eisenhower administration was engaged in a vicious "numbers game" to pad the statistics and make it appear that Republicans were tougher about firing Communists or Communist sympathizers. The Democrats claimed that many loyal government officials were being arbitrarily forced to resign to build the numbers against the Democrats.

When the Democrats won the 1954 election—and thus captured control of the congressional committees, they were eager to investigate and document the Democratic contention that the communists-in-government issue was "phony." Democratic committee members asked for records that they believed would prove their case, but they ran into a thick wall of secrecy.

The extreme campaign oratory and pledges had inflamed

the issue, and it was difficult to get it into perspective. There was no doubt of laxity in the administration of the security programs by some agencies, and the conviction of Alger Hiss on a perjury charge had made it appear to some Republicans that they were fully justified in charging that the Democrats as a whole were "soft" on Communists. Hiss had certainly held a key role in the State Department under the Democratic administrations, prior to exposure of his communist connections by the House Un-American Activities Committee in 1948.

Most Republican political figures took a fairly balanced view of the communists-in-government issue. They regarded the administration of loyalty-security programs as a difficult problem for any political party. They saw the need for some personnel changes and a little tighter administration of loyalty-security matters.

But the Republican party also harbored a few overeager, inexperienced, and a few downright malicious men who tackled the job of personnel security with a wild, free-swinging vigor and little real judgment. There was a little evidence in 1953 and 1954 of Republican mismanagement of some security cases. However, no real tangible evidence surfaced until January 1955, when Senator Olin D. Johnston, the South Carolina Democrat, and his Committee Staff Director H. William Brawley started an investigation of the security program. Johnston was chairman of the Senate Post Office and Civil Service Committee with jurisdiction over government personnel policies.

The investigation had barely started when the Eisenhower administration sought to hide the bungling and incompetence by claiming "executive privilege." By the time the hearings had been concluded in the following fall, the secrecy wall of "executive privilege" had been used by the State Department, the Agriculture Department, the Civil Service Commission, and the White House. A conspiracy of silence hampered the investigation from start to finish, but I had obtained enough information on one celebrated security case to demonstrate the kinds of mistakes and mismanagement generally involved.

In December 1954 and January 1955, I had written a series of articles describing the Agriculture Department's unjustified ruling on Wolf Ladejinsky. Ladejinsky, an agricultural attaché in Tokyo, was called a "security risk" by Agriculture Secretary Ezra Taft Benson without the slightest evidence that Ladejinsky's loyalty was questionable. The State Department had previously cleared Ladejinsky following an exhaustive investigation under the new and tighter security standards established by the Eisenhower administration.

I had been able to verify that the Agriculture Department made its adverse ruling on the same evidence that had been examined by the State Department when it cleared Ladejinsky. Harold Stassen, then head of the Foreign Operations Administration, moved in quickly to clear Ladejinsky. His report on Ladejinsky's file stated that there was no evidence that Ladejinsky had ever been sympathetic to any communist causes in the nineteen years he had been employed as an economist by the government.

Even with FOA and State on record clearing Ladejinsky, it took more than six months of congressional investigation to force Agriculture Secretary Benson to withdraw his finding that Ladejinsky was a "security risk." Throughout the entire period of time, the investigating subcommittee was obstructed by the refusal of various agencies to submit reports and give testimony.

Philip Young, chairman of the Civil Service Commission, refused to comply with a *subpoena duces tecum,* for production of records. He cited the May 17, 1954, letter on "executive privilege" and commented:

"The President's letter points out that it is essential to efficient and effective administration that employes of the ex-

ecutive branch be in a position to be completely candid in
advising each other on official matters, and that it is not in
the public interest that any of our conversations or communications or any documents or reproductions concerning such
advice be disclosed. . . ."

R. W. Scott McLeod, who then headed the State Department personnel security program, refused to tell the investigating subcommittee of his conversations with Milan D.
Smith, executive assistant to Agriculture Secretary Benson.
He claimed that to tell what he told Smith on the Ladejinsky
case would reveal advice within the executive branch of the
government, and would violate President Eisenhower's instructions on "executive privilege."

The report of the subcommittee of the Senate Post Office
and Civil Service Committee released on July 22, 1956, de-
voted an entire section to the problem of obtaining information from the executive branch in the face of the arbitrary
secrecy policies being used under a claim of "executive
privilege."

"At the outset and throughout the period of its existence
the subcommittee and staff have been handicapped in their
work by the refusal of the various executive agencies to submit files, upon written request or by subpena, which files had
a bearing upon the operation of the Government employees'
security program, the very subject designated to the subcommittee to investigate," the official subcommittee report
stated.

"Must the Congress set up its own investigational staff
with undercover men in various agencies so as to know what
goes on?" the subcommittee asked.

The report continued: "The legislative function cannot be
carried on in the dark. The Supreme Court has approved the
comment of Woodrow Wilson who said:

" 'It is the proper duty of a representative body to look
diligently into every affair of Government and to talk much

about what it sees. It is meant to be the eyes and the voice and to embody the wisdom and will of its constituents. Unless the Congress have and use every means of acquainting itself with the acts and the disposition of the administrative agents of the Government, the country must be helpless to learn how it is being served; and unless Congress both scrutinize these things and sift them by every form of discussion, the country must remain in embarrassing, crippling ignorance of the very affairs which it is most important that it should understand and direct.'"

The Johnston subcommittee declared that the interpretation being placed on the President's May 17, 1954, letter was such "as to force the Congress to legislate in a vacuum. Each department or agency head is the arbiter of what he should disclose, and in some instances disclosures were made when they reflected a credit on the department or agency or discredit on a committee witness."

Once again officials had testified freely on matters that made the political party or agency look good, but refused to produce records that might embarrass them.

The report cited the classic legal treatise, *Wigmore on Evidence*. In this work Professor Wigmore denies that the Chief Executive or any other officer has a testimonial privilege not to be a witness in court.

"The public (in the words of Lord Hardwicke) has a right to every man's evidence," Professor Wigmore wrote. "Is there any reason why this right should suffer an exemption when the desired knowledge is in the possession of a person occupying at the moment the office of the Chief Executive of a State?

"There is no reason at all. His temporary duties as an official cannot override his permanent and fundamental duty as a citizen and as a debtor to justice. The general principle . . . of testimonial duty to disclose Knowledge needed in judicial investigations is of universal force. It does not suffer an exception which would be irrespective of the nature of the person's Knowledge and would rest wholly in the nature of the person's occupation . . .

"Let it be understood then, that there is no exemption for officials as such, or for the Executive as such, from the universal testimonial duty to give evidence in judicial investigations. The exemptions that exist are defined by other principles."

The Johnston subcommittee report also made note of the act of the First Congress establishing the Treasury Department. This law made it the duty of the Secretary of the Treasury to "report and give information to either branch of the Legislature, in person or in writing (as may be required) respecting all matters referred to him by the Senate or House of Representatives, or which shall appertain to his office. . . ."

The subcommittee did not contend that it could force the President or cabinet officers to testify on any subject, but it did contend that cabinet officers must testify when there is a specific statute covering their responsibility.

Attention was called to the Supreme Court ruling in the famous case of *McGrain v. Daugherty,* handed down in 1927 in connection with the Senate investigation of the Teapot Dome scandals. The opinion written by Justice Van Devanter stated:

"We are of the opinion that the power of inquiry—with process to enforce it—is an essential and appropriate auxiliary to the legislative function. . . . A legislative body cannot legislate wisely or effectively in the absence of information respecting the conditions which the legislation is intended to affect or change; and where the legislative body does not itself possess the requisite information—which not infrequently is true—recourse must be had to others who do possess it. . . . Thus there is ample warrant for thinking, as we do, that the constitutional provisions which commit the legislative function to the two Houses are intended to include this attribute to the end that the function may be effectively exercised."

According to the best authorities it seemed clear that Congress had the power to compel testimony when searching for facts within its jurisdiction. The Supreme Court had held that private persons could be compelled to testify, and it seemed equally clear that government officials could be compelled to give evidence. There was no way for Congress to force the President personally to give testimony or produce records except by impeaching him. Yet he was obligated, along with all other government officials, to give testimony or produce records for a proper congressional committee as long as the national security was not endangered.

Certainly the revelation of testimony of conversations between a State Department personnel officer and an Agriculture Department personnel officer on the Wolf Ladejinsky case would not endanger the national security of the United States. It is significant that the Department of Agriculture departed from precedent in previous security cases in making information on Ladejinsky available, but this was information derogatory to Ladejinsky. The Department used secrecy to hide its own faulty administration. The claim of "executive privilege" was simply being used to cover up, and everyone familiar with the record knew it.

CHAPTER VIII

Secrecy Hides the Security Bunglers

By the spring of 1955, enough executive agencies were refusing records to Congress that Representative William Dawson, the Illinois Democrat who served as chairman of the House Government Operations Committee, had become concerned.

On June 9, 1955, Representative Dawson wrote to Representative John E. Moss, the young California Democrat, formally establishing a Government Information Subcommittee and asking that Moss be chairman. Congressman Moss was only in his second term in Congress, and normally would not have been assigned chairmanship of a subcommittee unless it appeared relatively unimportant as a vehicle for publicity.

"Charges have been made that Government agencies have denied or withheld pertinent and timely information to the newspapers, to radio, and television broadcasters, magazines, and other communication media, to trained and qualified research experts and to the Congress," Congressman Dawson wrote.

"An informed public makes the difference between mob rule and democratic government. If the pertinent and necessary information on governmental activities is denied the public, the result is a weakening of the democratic process and the ultimate atrophy of our form of government."

Moss took the assignment immediately but waited five

months before starting what was to become the committee's five-year struggle with the Eisenhower administration.

Although the investigation ultimately became involved almost exclusively in trying to break down the barrier of "executive privilege," it started out on general information policy problems. At the time of the first hearing (November 5, 1955) there was only a handful of observers greatly concerned over "executive privilege." James S. Pope, executive editor of the Louisville *Courier-Journal*, J. Russell Wiggins, executive editor of the Washington *Post and Times Herald*, and Harold L. Cross, special counsel for the American Society of Newspaper Editors, were among those who shared my worry.

James (Scotty) Reston, Washington correspondent for The New York *Times*, had recently expressed concern over "managed news." He objected to "the conscious effort" to give news emanating from the Geneva Conference "an optimistic" flavor.

"After the Geneva smiling, the new word went out that it might be a good idea now to frown a little bit, so the President made a speech at Philadelphia, taking quite a different light about the Geneva Conference," Reston said. "That is what I mean by managing the news."

I didn't like "managed news" any better than Reston, but I believed that the arbitrary secrecy of "executive privilege" was the core of the problem. There would be "managed news" as long as executive departments and independent regulatory agencies were able to invoke an arbitrary secrecy to prevent the press and Congress from reviewing the record—and as long as newspapers indolently accepted the management.

The Moss subcommittee gave me an excellent chance to state my views the first day of its hearings. I began my testimony with a review of the history of the May 17, 1954, letter and the Army-McCarthy hearings.

"Since that time," I stated, "seventeen departments of the Government have used this letter as a precedent for withholding actual decisions of the government. Conversations and documents used in arriving at decisions are regarded as confidential, and the Congress and reporters alike are denied information."

I pointed out that the American Civil Liberties Union had filed a complaint against the use of "executive privilege" by subordinates of executive agencies. And I commented that it was startling to find Senator McCarthy and the American Civil Liberties Union together on an issue.

"I think this demonstrates that this is not something political," I said. "The party in power may gain some kind of a temporary advantage from hiding the record, but in a long-time advantage, for both parties, it is best to try to make a full disclosure of what goes on in government."

In answer to questions I said I did not object to specific legislation to cover areas of government where secrecy was essential. I emphasized that "if the record of the government must be confidential, it is not too much to ask the executive department to give a reason. Democrats and Republicans in Congress have an equal interest in obtaining . . . the whole story, all of the information behind the decisions of the executive agency."

The next week, the Moss subcommittee on Government Information began calling the long roll of witnesses from the Post Office Department, the Agriculture Department, the Treasury Department, and the Civil Service Commission. The first task was to try to establish from reports and testimony just what the information practices of each of these departments were.

A few months of work revealed to Chairman Moss and his staff a tendency toward "a flexible policy" in many departments. A department might refuse to produce information on one ground, and then jump to another reason when the first became untenable. I knew that some press officials were poorly schooled as to what should and should not be made available, and that they made up the rules as they went along. If the Moss subcommittee had done no more than establish a written record on the laws and regulations being used for information policies its effort would have been worthwhile. Fortunately it did a lot more.

By the end of the first week of hearings the subcommittee staff (Staff Director Samuel J. Archibald, Chief Counsel Wallace J. Parks, and Special Counsel Jacob Scher) had already gathered a large collection of rules and regulations on information. Also, they had inserted in the record a copy of a Joint Resolution, No. 342, passed by the House of Representatives on May 13, 1948—a not-so-gentle reminder.

The Republican Eightieth Congress of 1948 had been so irritated at the Truman administration for its refusal to make records available to Congress that it passed a resolution directing "all executive departments and agencies of the Federal Government created by Congress" to furnish "such information, books, records and memoranda" as was demanded by a majority vote in any properly authorized committee of Congress.

At the time of that dispute in 1948, such leading Democrats as John W. McCormack, of Massachusetts, and William L. Dawson, of Illinois, defended the Truman administration for refusing to make available a Commerce Department investigative report on Dr. Edward U. Condon, director of the National Bureau of Standards.

President Truman had issued an executive order in which he stated that "efficient and just administration of the employee loyalty program . . . requires that reports, records, and files relative to the program be preserved in strict confidence."

Even though this was a specific executive order, and limited to investigative reports and personnel files, the Republicans were outraged at being denied access to all information on cases under investigation by Congress.

However, in 1955, when the tables had turned, the Republicans used the same basic arguments the Democrats used in 1948. The Republicans, moreover, were having to defend a far more widespread withholding of records.

During this dispute, I examined the 1948 records of the Senate on an investigation of a loyalty case involving William Remington, another Commerce Department official. William P. Rogers had been chief counsel for the committee investigating the Remington case, and had been in charge of preparing the Senate subcommittee report that castigated the Truman administration for arbitrary and unjustified secrecy in withholding personnel investigation files. In those reports, Rogers had likened withholding information from Congress to keeping the seeing-eye dog from a blind man.

This was the same William P. Rogers who was appointed Deputy Attorney General in the first term of the Eisenhower administration, and who later became the Attorney General and the leading spokesman for the ultimate in "executive privilege."

In his early days in the Justice Department, I saw Bill Rogers on a number of occasions and pointed out the inconsistency of his positions. I asked him how he could be such a caustic critic of secrecy in the Truman administration, and then suddenly switch to being a leading advocate of such total arbitrary secrecy as used by the Eisenhower administration in its stretched claim of "executive privilege."

"When you can show me that some crime or wrongdoing is being covered up, come up and see me," Rogers said.

I tried to reason with him, explaining that there were no laws and no judicial decisions to support so absurd a claim to an arbitrary right to withhold information. Rogers became jocular and said I was taking the whole business too seriously. He said that if there were serious cases he would examine them. He laughed off my suggestion that the cases then available were serious and some day in the future could be used as precedent to bury Democratic scandals from Republicans.

Rogers said that newspaper editorials had been in favor of the May 17, 1954, letter when it was issued, and that there was little support on my side. I stuck to my argument that he was contradicting his own position of six or seven years earlier. But it was no use to try to argue with him. I left him to do his explaining later to the Moss subcommittee and other congressional committees.

On May 8, 1956, the Moss subcommittee on Government Information heard testimony from Bernard Schwartz, professor of law and director of the Institute of Comparative Law at New York University; Hugh Fulton, former chief counsel for the Truman committee; and Harold L. Cross, special counsel for the American Society of Newspaper Editors.

Fulton, after an exhaustive statement on the problem of arbitrary withholding by the executive agencies, concluded that the efforts to impair the investigative power of Congress "hampers the legislative powers and imperils democracy as we know it."

Harold Cross, who had been practicing law since 1912, had also served for twenty-five years as a professor of newspaper law in the Graduate School of Journalism, Columbia University. I had known him for some years through work on projects for the American Society of Newspaper Editors.

In his testimony, Cross struck at the legal basis of the memorandum of Attorney General Herbert Brownell that had accompanied the May 17, 1954, letter.

"Some of the findings of the memorandum . . . are accurate," Cross said. [But] "the underlined part of the statement is merely an assertion by the Attorney General. It is at direct variance with pertinent court rulings.

"These cases, and others, are cited to this subcommittee as blanket authority for withholding information. They are cited as establishing in Federal officials, subordinates as well as heads, an inherent right to withhold information— not only from the public and press and individual Congressmen, but also from Congress itself and its committees. They are cited as establishing rights to withhold that are final and not subject to judicial review.

"Moreover," Cross said, "these Attorney General opinions, which cite no judicial authority, are inaccurate, are at direct variance with pertinent court rulings."

Cross concluded that Brownell's "inaccurate" legal rulings "are both cited and applied as if they were Holy Writ to suppress information which this Congress needs in order to legislate, which the press needs in order to perform its functions and which citizens need in order to maintain a self-governing society."

It was inspiring to have such a clear statement and such an exhaustive study from Harold Cross. He was highly respected by the editors of the American Society of Newspaper Editors, and I was certain that his logic would soon convince many editors of the wisdom of a united opposition to the unbridled claim of "executive privilege."

Now came my first meeting with Bernard Schwartz, then only thirty-three years old but already a recognized authority in the fields of constitutional and administrative law. The testimony of this short, dark-haired professor with the heavy glasses was clear, well documented, restrained. His condemnation of the May 17, 1954, letter was altogether effective.

The letter claimed, Schwartz said, that the executive agencies had "the absolute privilege and discretion" to withhold information from Congress and the public.

"Those who assert that the law is settled in favor of an unlimited right in the Executive . . . do so out of an excess of executive zeal but without any real basis in fact, or in law for that matter.

"There is no statute or judicial decision which justifies the extreme pretensions of privilege consistently maintained by executive officials," Schwartz said.

"It is true that there is a long history of executive refusals to comply with congressional investigative demands and that these refusals have often been justified, upon supposed legal grounds, by opinions of the Attorney General," he continued. "Neither opinions of the Attorney General nor the practice of the Executive can justify unwarranted distortions of the Constitution. . . . Nor does a governmental practice conceived in error become elevated to the plane of legality merely because the error has been long persisted in."

Schwartz called attention to arguments that Congress was abusing its investigative power, and commented: "To this writer, indeed, the overriding danger is not Congressional abuse but the vesting of unfettered discretion in the Executive to surround with secrecy all its activities.

"Those who are concerned with the possibility of legislative abuse ignore the overriding peril of the present century, that [of] the superstate with its omnipotent administration, unrestrained by any checks on its all-pervasive regulatory activities, so vividly pictured by George Orwell in his novel *1984*.

"The great danger today is 1984, not Senator McCarthy. If the elected representatives of the people assert their right to lay bare all that goes on within the Executive, that danger may be avoided. An Executive whose abuses and inadequacies are exposed to the public eye can hardly become a menace to constitutional government."

There had never been any doubt in my mind about the basic problems involved in the executive claim of an unlimited right to withhold information. But it was comforting to be supported by the exhaustive legal studies of Fulton, Cross, and Schwartz.

This was only the start of an interesting association with Professor Schwartz, who later became a headline figure as a result of his controversial investigation of the independent regulatory agencies.

CHAPTER IX

Secrecy Curtain on Iron Curtain Deals

While the Moss investigations continued, the Senate Permanent Investigating Subcommittee was accumulating evidence that showed how a relaxation of government controls over shipments of vital and strategic materials had resulted in a sharply increased flow of these materials to the Soviet-bloc countries. In February 1956, Chairman John L. McClellan, the Arkansas Democrat, opened public hearings on the relaxation of controls over East-West trade.

McClellan announced that his staff—headed by Chief Counsel Robert F. Kennedy and Investigator LaVern Duffy —had discovered "evidence that merchants of the free world are helping to build up Russia's military potential by furnishing it items which are indispensable in constructing or maintaining a war machine."

In August 1954, representatives of the North Atlantic Treaty Organization nations, plus Japan, had met in Paris in a Coordinating Committee known as COCOM. This committee had downgraded, or otherwise decontrolled, approximately 150 out of 450 strategic items. Items removed from the embargo list included heavy metal-working machinery, electric power generating equipment, minerals, metals, transportation equipment, and petroleum products and equipment.

"Such downgrading and removal [from embargo lists] has

been harmful to the security of the non-Communist world," Chairman McClellan said.

Chief Counsel Kennedy tried to push into the U.S. Government agencies to find out how this relaxation had taken place, and to pin down the responsibility for the action. Excuses of security were given to refuse information, and there were claims that testimony by U.S. officials might interfere with our relations with our allies. When such excuses failed to stand up, the blanket arbitrary secrecy of "executive privilege" was invoked to hide disputes that had taken place in government on the revision of the strategic materials list.

The committee was forced to rely on testimony from persons no longer in government, or on tips from persons in government who contacted investigators quietly because they feared losing their jobs if they co-operated openly.

Thanks to such testimony, it soon became apparent who had changed the strategic materials list to permit shipment of copper, aluminum, precision boring machines, and huge horizontal boring and drilling and milling machines to Iron Curtain countries.

"The downgrading and decontrol of approximately 150 of the items," the McClellan subcommittee reported, "were recommended by personnel in our own Government agencies on the so-called Joint Operating Committees, contrary to advice of the experts and technicians of the Defense Department and in many instances against the advice of experts in their own agencies."

There were indications at an early stage of the investigations that the revisions in the embargo list made the whole strategic list a complete farce. Simple jig boring machines were retained on the list as being prohibited from shipment to a potential enemy. However, the revised list allowed the shipment of more modern precision boring machines of much higher strategic value.

Initially the Eisenhower administration policy was not unified in barring access to testimony and records. But, as the subcommittee intensified its investigation, the requests for information ran into a stone wall of opposition from the executive agencies involved—the State Department, Defense Department, Commerce Department, and the Foreign Operations Administration. No one claimed that defense secrets were involved. The executive branch abandoned any pretense and fell back on the arbitrary refusal by simply citing President Eisenhower's May 17, 1954, letter.

The arrogance of the executive branch was best demonstrated by the letter from Secretary of Commerce Sinclair Weeks to Commerce Department employees. He wrote:

"You are instructed not to testify either in public or executive closed session with respect to any advice, recommendations, discussions and communications within the executive branch respecting any course of action in regard to East-West trade control or as to any information regarding international negotiation with the countries cooperating in East-West trade controls. . . ."

Weeks tried to give some color of law to the claim of executive secrecy by citing three federal court cases, but the subcommittee declared none of the cases cited involved the right to withhold information from congressional committees.

It was Harold Stassen, then a Special Assistant to the President, who balked at giving information in a manner that most galled the subcommittee members.

"Are you willing to give us full, detailed, and complete information?" Chairman McClellan asked Stassen.

Stassen replied: "I am willing to give you, and the executive branch is willing to give you, every bit of information that does not violate one of three considerations: One, security from the standpoint of intelligence; two, the rule on internal executive branch documents . . . ; three, the details of international negotiations which would make our relations with our allies more difficult."

"Are you willing to give us the list of items that were de-controlled or downgraded?"

"No, I do not have . . . those lists now."

"All right," McClellan said. "Let me ask you: Are you permitted to testify under the security cloak that is wrapped around Government officials in this matter?"

Stassen declared that McClellan was helping the Communists in revealing material on the strategic materials list.

"You say I am helping the Communists," McClellan snapped. "The allies, whose position you are defending, Great Britain—I hope our strongest ally—publishes the list so the Communists can see what she will sell, the very items that are today classified from the Congress and the American people."

Stassen was surprised. "The United Kingdom does not publish the international list, Mr. Chairman, that I know of."

McClellan picked up some papers and extended them toward Stassen. "Here it is; I hold it in my hand. This is a Board of Trade *Journal*, October 16, 1954, on which wire, copper wire, is excluded, so they know they can buy it."

"Would you give it to me, please?" asked Stassen.

Even after Stassen was given the list published by the British, he refused to make the almost identical American list available to the McClellan subcommittee. After a long and unsuccessful effort to obtain information from Stassen, Senator Sam Ervin concluded that the Eisenhower administration was willing to talk a lot but say nothing.

In his slow North Carolina drawl, the gray-haired Democrat elaborated:

"We have had experience here that people in the lower echelons of the executive departments have had their mouths stopped, and we were told that those who were at the higher levels could give us information. But I have come to this conclusion: That our position is sort of like that of one of my clients, who came in my office one day and said that he wanted to get a divorce from his wife.

"He admitted she was a good woman, a good mother, and a good housekeeper. I said, 'Well, what in the world do you want to get a divorce from her for?' He said, 'Well, she just talks, and talks, and talks, and talks, and talks all the time.' I said, 'What does she talk about?' And he said, 'Well, she don't say.'"

Stassen's refusal to say anything was made all the more appalling by the publication of *The Inside Story*, a book about the Eisenhower administration written by Robert J. Donovan of the New York *Herald Tribune*.

"The contents of the book," the McClellan subcommittee stated, "are based upon documents, materials, minutes, and other information similar in nature and character to that which this subcommittee has been trying to obtain in the course of discharging its legislative duties and responsibilities.

"The executive branches of the Government have been adamant in refusing to make such information available to this subcommittee, and it is difficult to reconcile such attitude with its willingness to give similar information to private individuals."

The McClellan subcommittee was not critical of Donovan, but the members were infuriated by the policy inconsistencies. A request was made for Maxwell Rabb, Cabinet Secretary, to appear and explain the reasons and circumstances surrounding the release of information to Donovan.

"Rabb failed and refused to appear," the subcommittee reported. "Thereafter, a letter was sent to Under Secretary of State [Herbert] Hoover [Jr.], Secretary of Commerce [Sinclair] Weeks, ICA Director [John B.] Hollister, Assistant Secretary of Defense Gordon Gray, calling attention to the fact that material of a confidential nature and relating to the internal workings of the government at Cabinet and staff levels had been disclosed to a private individual for a commercial purpose, and in the light of these facts, the chairman of the subcommittee again requested that the documents of the Joint Operating Committee, relating to decontrol of strategic materials, be made available to this subcommittee as early as possible."

The information was not supplied, and the McClellan subcommittee declared that this "suppression of information raises not only the question as to the right of Congress to know, but also the question of the right of the public in a democracy to be informed as to the activities of its government."

In its reports, the McClellan subcommittee declared that the doctrine of separation of powers as explained in President Eisenhower's May 17, 1954, letter was totally wrong in asserting the complete independence of the executive branch. The subcommittee quoted from the opinion of Chief Justice William Howard Taft in the Grossman case in which he said:

"Complete independence and separation between the three branches, however, are not attained or intended, as other provisions of the Constitution and the normal operation of government under it easily demonstrate." The Grossman case set out the various checks the executive, legislative, and judicial departments are specifically granted under the Constitution.

The subcommittee legal report stated flatly that there are no legal cases upholding the claimed "inherent right to withhold information" from Congress.

In another report, the subcommittee also challenged the broad use of the May 17, 1954, letter from Eisenhower to Defense Secretary Wilson. The report quoted from the May 17, 1954, letter:

"You will instruct employees of your Department that in

all their appearances before the subcommittee of the Senate Committee on Government Operation regarding the inquiry now before it [Army-McCarthy hearings] they are not to testify. . . ."

"It is clear that this letter was intended to apply specifically to the Army-McCarthy hearings," the subcommittee report concluded, but the fact was that it had "been cited by twenty or more federal agencies and departments as grounds for refusing information to Congress."

Chairman McClellan went on the Senate floor to express his concern over the total secrecy that was being clamped on the executive branch.

"The Government agencies acting in concert are doing everything to hinder and hamper the Subcommittee's efforts to ascertain the facts concerning the relaxation of these controls," the Senator declared. "Except for some cooperation from the Department of Defense, the information has not been forthcoming. The facts the Subcommittee has developed thus far . . . have not been made available or furnished . . . by the executive agencies.

"The information we have has been secured from documents and publications of foreign governments, where the information is being freely given out by our allies. That same information in the United States is being withheld by the executive branch of our Government from both the Congress and the American people."

McClellan declared it is "a farce" how the Battle Act list of strategic materials is withheld from Congress and the people of the United States but is available to the Communist-bloc countries. "They know what they can buy," he said. "They [the Communist bloc countries] know what they do buy and have bought.

"Can it be . . . this classification, this policy of secrecy, this suppression or withholding of the truth is a process or an action designed for hiding of errors, inefficiency and bad

judgment of Government officials?" he asked. "I am convinced it is. If not, then why not give the Congress the information and let the American people know the truth?"

Senator Richard Russell, the veteran Georgia Democrat,
joined McClellan in denouncing the arbitrary secrecy in
the East-West trade investigations. He said it presented "a
very shocking picture of the failure of cooperation with the
Congress in a field in which we have as direct a responsibility
or a greater responsibility than the executive department in
attempting to maintain a superiority in arms, in order that
we may defend our country."

Senator Wayne Morse, the Oregon Democrat, also lashed
out at the secrecy, and declared that such hiding of government records would justify voting against the whole foreign-
aid program.

"We have a right to know what goods foreign-aid countries
ship to Russia," Morse said. "We are not asking for the disclosure of secrets which involve the war plans of our country,
[and] which should be kept secret."

Senator Joseph R. McCarthy and Senator Morse were
rarely together on an issue. But on the question of secrecy
in the Eisenhower administration, Senator McCarthy lined
up with Morse, McClellan, Russell, and such liberals as
Senator Paul Douglas (Dem., Ill.) and Senator Thomas
Hennings (Dem., Mo.).

"I was extremely critical of the Democrat administration
for withholding information from Congress," McCarthy said
in a Senate speech. "During the hearings which the very
able Senator from Arkansas has been conducting, I was
appalled by the even greater secrecy maintained by the
executive branch today. As the years go by the Executive is
becoming more and more arrogant and highhanded toward
legitimate congressional requests for information."

By this time I was starting to feel optimistic about breaking
the secrecy barrier, for it seemed that political figures of all

complexions were aroused about the danger it created for a democratic government. Additionally, at this time there came a report, dated May 3, 1956, from the House Government Operations Committee, parent of the Moss subcommittee. It stated that the Eisenhower administration's claim to an inherent right to secrecy "has never been upheld by the courts. It has been a mere Executive *ipse dixit* [say so]."

The five-point conclusion of this report seemed to me to be as fine a résumé of the legal situation as I had seen:

"1. Refusals by the President and heads of departments to furnish information to the Congress are not constitutional law. They represent a mere naked claim of privilege. The judiciary has never specifically ruled on the direct problem involved in a refusal by Federal agencies to furnish information to the Congress.

"2. As far as access to information is concerned the courts have not distinguished basically between executive agencies and quasi-legislative or quasi-judicial agencies. Both appear to stand in the same status.

"3. Judicial precedent shows that even the President has been held to be subject to the power of subpena of the courts. While this is so, it may be that the only recourse against the President himself is impeachment if he fails to comply with a subpena of either the courts or the Congress.

"4. Any possible presidential immunity from the enforcement of legal process does not extend to the heads of departments and other Federal agencies. Judicial opinions have never recognized any inherent right in the heads of Federal agencies to withhold information from the courts. The courts have stated that even where the head of the department or agency bases his action on statutory authority the courts will judge the reasonableness of the action in the same light as any other claim of privilege. The courts have held that the mere claim of privilege is not enough.

"5. There is no inherent right on the part of heads of the

departments or other Federal agencies to withhold information from the Congress any more than they have a right to withhold information from the Judiciary. . . ."

Before the McClellan subcommittee on the Senate side completed its report, a number of voices had been raised in defense of the Eisenhower administration's secrecy. But they did not seem to be strong voices. Only Senator Karl E. Mundt, the South Dakota Republican, and George H. Bender, the Ohio Republican, signed a minority report on the East-West trade investigation.

Senator Mundt and Senator Bender charged that the report of the five-member majority "is entirely misleading as to the effectiveness of international control of strategic materials." Although Chairman McClellan had consistently indicated a willingness to take testimony or records in a closed session if a problem of real national security was involved, Mundt and Bender defended the Eisenhower administration's refusal to make information available on grounds that to testify might help the Communists.

"To make some of this information available in public session would tell the Communist nations about our strategic and short supply, reason for control and decontrol," the Mundt-Bender report stated. "We would publicize for the benefit of potential enemies the thoughts, recommendations, advice and working papers of subordinates who worked for those in the executive branch who held and exercised action responsibility."

In years past, Senator Mundt had been highly critical of the secrecy of the Truman administration. Now, however, he said he wished to "disassociate myself from that conclusion" by Senator McClellan that secrecy is being used to cover up "errors, inefficiency and bad judgment."

"I think at the moment it is purely a political deduction," Senator Mundt said.

Hardly anyone took Senator Bender's position seriously for he was generally regarded as a political buffoon. To discredit his support of the Eisenhower administration's secrecy, the majority report merely quoted from two speeches that Bender had made as a House member in October 1951.

In October 1951, when the shoe had been on the other foot, Bender rose on two occasions to castigate the Truman administration for a censorship of government information.

"Power over the press," he said, "is the path to dictatorship."

And:

"What most of us find the most objectionable in the President's [Truman's] order is the ease with which it can be used to cover up blunders and incompetence, and the absence of any provision for removing secrecy provisions after the emergency has passed. We may now find our friends in other countries revealing information which we are not permitted to publish or broadcast."

Bender's last sentence could not have been more prophetic. The majority report hammered home the prophecy-come-true: "The British have published substantially the same export-control list as that which our Government departments and agencies seek to hide and conceal from the American people."

On the basis of consistency, reason, and logic the Eisenhower administration's broad use of "executive privilege" was by now thoroughly discredited. I did not see how President Eisenhower or anyone else could defend it, but I had not taken into account President Eisenhower's lack of understanding of just what was taking place under the cover of "executive privilege." The President was exceedingly popular, and there were plenty of people who were willing to use his good name and reputation for honesty as a cover for their own errors, incompetence, misjudgments, or improprieties.

CHAPTER X

Pressing a Point with Ike

The final reports from the four congressional investigations —a House Government Operations Committee, the Senate Dixon-Yates investigating subcommittee, the McClellan subcommittee on East-West trade, and the Wolf Ladejinsky probe—were all released during the summer of 1956. Each assailed the excessive arbitrary secrecy that had hampered the investigations.

So, once again, at a press conference on September 27, 1956, I raised the problem of arbitrary executive secrecy with President Eisenhower.

"Mr. President," I said. "At least four Congressional committees in a period of the last few weeks have issued reports that were critical of what they termed excessive secrecy which they felt covered up mismanagement in the operation of the Government.

"Now, these committees contend that there is no court decision backing the broad proposition of executive secrecy, and I wondered if you could tell us if you feel that all employees of the Federal Government, at their own discretion, can determine whether they will testify or will not testify before committees when there is no security problem involved?"

The President's answer indicated that he was still not aware of the scope of the problem.

"Well, I believe that the instructions are clear, that when

there is no question of security, national security, involved, that everybody is supposed to testify freely before congressional committees. I will have to look up the regulations, I mean the letters of instruction that have gone out. Primarily, I think this is a function of the department heads and the separate office heads—"

"Well, Mr. President—" I tried to break in to correct him, but he continued.

"I don't believe that any individual who happens to be, let's say from a filing clerk on up can by themselves decide what is right for them to tell and what is not right."

"Mr. President," I explained. "They used the May 17, 1954, letter that you wrote to Secretary Wilson in the Army-McCarthy hearings as a precedent in this particular case. I wonder if you felt they were misusing it if they use it, say, a clerk or an assistant secretary?"

The President was mildly irked at being pressed to comment on a specific situation. "Now, you give me a very long and involved and detailed question here at a place where I don't even remember what I wrote to Secretary Wilson at that time. I will have to look it up. If you will put your question . . . in to Mr. Hagerty so we can look it up, why, it will be answered."

I was amazed that the President didn't have a better grasp of the problem at this late date. Dozens of government officials had been using his name and his letter to Wilson as a justification for refusing to produce records in a number of cases which had been headline news, but he couldn't remember what his policy was.

On leaving the press conference, I returned to the National Press Building and prepared my question for submission to Jim Hagerty. I drafted the question with care so there could be no confusion as to the points at issue, and delivered it to Hagerty at the White House. The letter follows.

Mr. President: At least four congressional committees have issued reports recently criticizing the executive agencies for what they term "excessive secrecy" that can cover up mismanagement.

These committees contend that there are no court decisions to support the broad contention of the "confidential executive business" as set forth in your May 17, 1954, letter to Secretary Wilson in the Army-McCarthy hearings.

The committees do not quarrel with your personal right to declare specific acts or communications as "confidential." They do argue that many subordinate officials are wrongfully using the May 17, 1954, letter to claim that their government actions and communications are "confidential."

Some agencies have stated that Congress is entitled to "only final decisions" of the agency, and has no right of access to papers leading up to the decisions.

Do you feel that all employees of the Executive Branch have the discretion to testify or not testify before Congress about their official acts, when no security is involved?

At what level does this discretion lodge?

If you feel this is a misuse of the precedent, would you clarify this matter on the access to information by the Congress and the press?

I knew the question would be answered by Gerald D. Morgan, the White House counsel, and I made several trips to the White House to convince him of the wisdom of limiting the use of "executive privilege" to cases approved specifically by the President.

Morgan seemed to be convinced at that stage that the Eisenhower administration should put some bridle on the unrestrained use of "executive privilege" by officials at all levels. I argued that it was to the advantage of the administration in power to have the congressional committees actively policing the agencies, and that there was grave danger of corruption developing in any agency where those in charge felt they could arbitrarily block congressional investigators.

Morgan asked that I send him a memorandum on the proper safeguards against improper use of "executive privilege." I felt optimistic when I submitted the memorandum to Morgan October 4, 1956, and felt that perhaps the Eisenhower administration was willing to take action publicly to end this arbitrary secrecy.

I had mentioned to Morgan that I had read the article he had written for the California *Law Review* of December 1949, in which he spoke forcefully in support of the power of Congress to compel testimony and production of records.

Morgan's article, entitled "Congressional Investigations and Judicial Review," was written when he was an assistant legislative counsel to the House of Representatives. In those years he had been a critic of the Truman administration for excessive secrecy and a strong advocate of the power of Congress to investigate.

In his law review article, Morgan pulled apart the Supreme Court decision in *Kilbourn v. Thompson,* a case decided in 1881. For years this case had cast some doubt on the rights of the Congress to conduct broad investigations to carry out its legislative function. Morgan pointed out that *Kilbourn v. Thompson* was a discredited decision, and that the 1927 case of *McGrain v. Daugherty* upheld the right of congressional committees to compel witnesses to testify and produce records.

The case of *McGrain v. Daugherty* arose out of the Teapot Dome scandal investigation of the 1920s. It was the same case that was cited by various congressional committees in 1956 as authority for insisting on testimony and records from government agencies.

The letter Gerald Morgan wrote me was not what I wanted,

and it certainly was inconsistent with the principles he had set forth in his 1949 law review article (see Appendix B). But it did demonstrate some desire to come to grips with the problem. He wrote:

"An employee is not free merely to exercise his own discretion (with regard to testimony and production of documents), but in the final analysis information will be withheld only when the President or agency heads acting under the President's authority or instruction determine it is contrary to the public interest to disclose it."

Inasmuch as the letter suggested that information should be given to committees of Congress unless there was a specific order to the contrary from the President, Congressman John Moss thought it portended an easing of the restrictions on information. At least he hoped it did. How futile was his hope we were soon to see.

Unfortunately, the Congress had to rely to a large extent on the Justice Department in normal moves to take court action against any government officials who refused to give testimony. So, although the case of *McGrain v. Daugherty* upheld the right of Congress to demand testimony and records, there was yet a practical problem involved. Congress had to depend on the good faith of the Attorney General and his top aides to enforce its demand.

A case in point occurred in the summer of 1956 when the Justice Department used the secrecy of "executive privilege" in an effort to block an investigation of a settlement of an antitrust suit. The antitrust suit involved American Telephone and Telegraph (A.T. & T.), and the investigation was being conducted by Representative Emanuel Celler's anti-monopoly subcommittee of the House Judiciary Committee. Chief Counsel Herbert Maletz was instructed by Celler to obtain the Justice Department files to determine the facts leading up to the settlement of the A.T. & T. antitrust suit.

The suit had been initiated by the Department in 1949 for

the purpose of forcing a divorce of A.T. & T. and its subsidiary, Western Electric. The separation was urged to break
the near monopoly that Western Electric enjoyed in the
production of telephone equipment.

The suit had been hailed by Attorney General Herbert
Brownell as a great victory for the government, but he and
Deputy Attorney General William P. Rogers claimed "executive privilege" and refused to make the files available. They
covered up the fact that the settlement allowing A.T. & T.
to continue the ties with Western Electric was made over
the opposition of staff members in the Justice Department.

Although Herbert Maletz was blocked from examining the
files of the Justice Department, he managed to obtain much
of the information he sought from the files of A.T. & T. and
from records in the Defense Department. This outside probe
uncovered some interesting things that Justice Department
secrecy had hidden. It showed that a high official of A.T. & T.
had written a letter which Defense Secretary Charles E.
Wilson sent to the Justice Department urging settlement of
the antitrust suit on terms favorable to A.T. & T. The investigation also revealed the conversations between Attorney
General Brownell and a lawyer for A.T. & T. that paved the
way to settlement.

Because "executive privilege" blocked the Celler subcommittee from questioning Justice Department employees, it
was necessary to subpoena a former official of the Justice
Department to establish that Brownell's settlement was actually opposed by the working staff in the Antitrust Division.
But who could override Brownell, the President's chief legal
adviser? The investigation stopped at the door of his office.

The Celler antimonopoly subcommittee of the House Judiciary Committee ran into "executive privilege" again when
it started to investigate the operations of the Business Advisory Committee (BAC) and the Department of Commerce.

Chairman Celler, an aggressive New York Democrat, was concerned over the way the BAC was influencing policy in the Department of Commerce. He questioned whether there were adequate safeguards against the misuse of such a committee. Without the safeguards, it could become a device for getting competitors together for price fixing or other violations of the antitrust laws.

Chief Counsel Maletz, under directions from Celler, asked for the minutes of the meetings of the BAC and the details of the operations. The subcommittee requests were rejected by Commerce Secretary Sinclair Weeks on grounds that the BAC minutes were "confidential" business of the executive branch of government.

Chairman Celler then argued that the BAC was a private committee, not supported by government funds and not a government agency. He denied that any "executive privilege" existed and declared that if it did exist, Secretary Weeks could not use it properly to try to cover up the activities of a private group that happened to give some advice to a department of government.

Commerce Secretary Weeks replied that BAC was a government committee, and that the minutes of BAC meetings therefore were covered by an "executive privilege."

Presumably the Celler antimonopoly subcommittee would have been allowed access to the minutes of the BAC if Weeks had considered it a private business group. But in order to put those minutes out of the reach of congressional inquiry Secretary Weeks was forced to the ludicrous position of claiming that the private group became a part of the government (and therefore entitled to an "executive privilege") merely by advising it.

I had often used a quotation from Patrick Henry in talks on secrecy, but it had never been more appropriate than now. Said Henry:

"To cover with the veil of secrecy the common routine of

business, is an abomination in the eyes of every intelligent man and every friend to his country."

I was reminded also of these telling words of Edward Livingston:

"No nation ever yet found any inconvenience from too close an inspection into the conduct of its officers. But many have been brought to ruin, and reduced to slavery, by suffering gradual imposition and abuses which were imperceptible only because the means of publicity had not been secured."

One could only wonder when President Eisenhower would awaken to the abuses of secrecy being perpetrated in his name, right under his own nose.

CHAPTER XI

Keeping the Professor in the Dark

The Justice Department, Commerce Department, Agriculture Department, Defense Department, and State Department had all used the arbitrary secrecy of "executive privilege" without causing a public uproar. Not only had they succeeded in avoiding major press criticism, but they had secured statements from President Eisenhower to give a noble and patriotic coloring to their deceptions.

With such encouragement at the top it was inevitable that the policy of secrecy would spread. In August 1957, the newly created House Legislative Oversight Subcommittee hired Bernard Schwartz, the young law professor from New York (see Chapter VIII), as counsel for an investigation of the various regulatory agencies. The committee, headed by Representative Morgan Moulder, Missouri Democrat, had been established "to go into the administration of the laws [creating the regulatory agencies] and see whether or not the laws . . . were being carried out or whether they were being repealed or revamped by those who administer them."

The young professor had barely started his work in September 1957, when he began bumping into secrecy trouble. In all, there were six of the so-called "independent regulatory agencies" in the scope of the House Legislative Oversight Subcommittee. The "big six" to be probed were the Federal Communications Commission (FCC), the Civil Aeronautics Board (CAB), the Interstate Commerce Commission (ICC), the Federal Power Commission (FPC), the Federal Trade Commission (FTC), and the Securities and Exchange Commission (SEC).

The Congress had created these regulatory agencies to perform a wide range of functions including control of radio and television licenses, control of gas and electric power lines, control of commercial land transportation by train, truck, or bus, the investment market, and air transportation. Rights worth billions of dollars were involved in the decisions of these agencies, and it had been the stated intention of Congress to remove these decisions from the direct pressure of politics. To do this, the regulatory agencies were headed by bipartisan commissions or boards, the members of which were nominated by the President, subject to approval by the Senate and limited to a fixed term of office.

In theory, at least, these boards or commissions were specialized courts in their fields. They had rule-making and administrative functions, but they also rendered judicial decisions on the basis of public records and public hearings. Once appointed, these members of the regulatory agencies were to be insulated from the pressure politics of the White House and the Congress. Prior to Dr. Schwartz's arrival in Washington, there had been widespread reports, and some evidence, that members of some of the regulatory commissions were engaging in conversations with political personnel at the White House and elsewhere on cases under study. To Dr. Schwartz, an outstanding authority in the field of administrative law, it was elementary that such conversations were improper while a case was being decided.

"It is as bad as having one of the parties in a law suit sneak into the chambers of the judge to try to influence his decision in the middle of a trial," Dr. Schwartz told me.

I discussed some incidents with him which I felt merited investigation, and he told me he was having trouble getting access to material he requested. The CAB appeared ready to try to pull down a secrecy curtain as broad as "executive privilege" because it could have no legal substance for an independent regulatory agency.

On September 19, Dr. Schwartz requested that the CAB allow members of the House subcommittee staff "to receive and examine any records, documents, or information directly, or indirectly, pertaining to your agency, function or business within the jurisdiction of this subcommittee."

A few days later, on September 23, he pressed CAB Chairman James R. Durfee for full access to CAB records. Durfee insisted the CAB would screen all files containing documents or communications from other agencies or departments of government. It was now apparent that Durfee was going to refuse access to internal governmental communications on grounds of "executive privilege." Dr. Schwartz was irate. He termed Chairman Durfee's position "completely ridiculous" and suggested that Durfee obtain competent legal counsel.

By this time the pressure of the investigation was being felt by a number of the regulatory agencies. The chairmen of the six regulatory agencies met at a luncheon at the University Club in Washington the next week to determine how to handle the inquisitive Dr. Schwartz. Because of the success some government departments had been having with "executive privilege" some of the chairmen decided that this was to be the answer for their agencies, but there was no general agreement.

Dr. Schwartz was not discouraged by the lack of information; he only pressed harder. Subcommittee Chairman Morgan Moulder took the suggestion of Dr. Schwartz and set October 17 as a public hearing date for CAB. In the meantime, on October 5, he followed another Schwartz suggestion and asked that the CAB prepare and submit a report on "all gifts, honorariums, loans, fees, or other payments" of things of value received by CAB employees from any "person, firms, corporation, association, organization, or group having any interest, direct or indirect," in any matter before the board.

Dr. Schwartz was allowed to examine the public files, but his efforts to obtain files of correspondence with the White House and with other agencies ran into the claim of "executive privilege." In the first months, he nevertheless became aware that Sherman Adams and others on the White House staff had been extremely active in reaching various regulatory agencies.

In an exhaustive eighty-two-page "Memorandum of Law," filed on October 17, Dr. Schwartz exposed the true nature of the "executive privilege" arguments. They all sprang from the idea that "the King can do no wrong."

"In the pretension of those who espouse 'executive privilege,'" he said, "the infallibility recognized in the King in the days when he was personally sovereign of England has been attributed to the President in our system. The reasoning which supports the doctrine should shock the intelligence, as well as the sense of justice, of those who truly believe in the essentials of representative democracy."

He reported that the CAB claimed "the authority to screen files and records before they are made available to the subcommittee, with a right to the Board in its discretion to remove any and all documents" that could be considered personal files of Board members or communications within CAB or with the White House.

"The Civil Aeronautics Board cannot claim privilege with regard to communication between the Board, on the one hand, and the President or other departments and agencies, on the other. Such an assertion of privilege cannot defeat the right of this subcommittee to investigate the relationship between the independent regulatory agencies and the executive branch."

Schwartz continued: "'Executive privilege' is not available to an independent agency like the Civil Aeronautics

Board as a possible basis for the withholding of information from the Congress. The Civil Aeronautics Board, as the Supreme Court has recognized, is an independent agency whose members are not subject to the removal power of the President. Such a body cannot in any proper sense be characterized as an arm or an eye of the Executive. It is instead an arm of the Congress, wholly responsible to that body.

"The doctrine of absolute 'executive privilege' itself is not supported in law. The cases cited by its proponents are not truly relevant on the power of the Executive to withhold information from the Congress. On the other hand, there are many decisions squarely rejecting the doctrine, even in courtroom cases. In addition, Dean Wigmore (the leading authority on the subject in this country) flatly repudiates the doctrine."

Although Dr. Schwartz did succeed in eliciting half-promises of co-operation from some officials of the regulatory agencies, most of them dragged their feet. Richard A. Mack, a member of the FCC, wouldn't show investigators many of his records, including the office diary that provided links for his indictment later on charges of having conspired to violate the federal law. The lack of co-operation by Commissioner Mack was matched by the resistance at CAB, where Schwartz was trying to pin down evidence of contacts by Sherman Adams.

In January 1958—after five months of frustration—Schwartz insisted that the members of the Legislative Oversight Subcommittee get tough and demand full co-operation. Some members of the investigating committee did not want to force the issue. Several of the Republicans came out flatly in support of the Eisenhower administration's obstructionist tactics.

The lack of support from committee members so irritated Schwartz that it took only a little urging from some newsmen to get him to leak a staff memorandum to The New York

Times. It was a lengthy document setting out the well-settled legal principle that it is improper for members of regulatory agencies to have private talks with litigants when a case is in hearing or in the process of being decided. The Schwartz memorandum also questioned the propriety of the members' accepting lavish entertainment from executives of the industries they were supposed to regulate.

Tempers flared in the days following the leak of the Schwartz memorandum, and finally on February 10, 1958, the House subcommittee voted to fire Dr. Schwartz. I called Dr. Schwartz in the early evening of February 10 to inform him of the subcommittee's decision and also to tell him that a subpoena was to be issued for him to testify the next morning.

He told me he had copies of every important document from the committee files in a trunk and two cardboard boxes. "Someone should have knowledge of what is in these records," he said, "so it will be possible to force the subcommittee to continue hearings." If something dramatic wasn't done, he was convinced the investigation would never get off the ground.

Dr. Schwartz asked if I wanted the copies of documents to take to members of Congress who had shown an interest in the problems of the regulatory agencies. I said I should not take possession of documents which might be considered the property of the House subcommittee. But since the documents were legally in his custody, I suggested that he could take them to the apartment of Senator John J. Williams, the Delaware Republican, and I would be happy to accompany him.

I had talked with Senator Williams of improper pressure on the regulatory agencies and thought he would take the records. He had fought against tax scandals in the Truman administration, but I regarded him as an objective crusader who would call the strikes the same way if the Eisenhower administration were involved in wrongdoing. I had hoped that Senator Williams might be able to give the investigation of regulatory agencies the same prodding that he had given to the House tax scandals investigations in 1951 and 1952.

Dr. Schwartz said he would be willing to turn the papers over to Senator Williams and explain them to him in detail.

I headed at once for his apartment. When I arrived, Dr. Schwartz had the trunk and two boxes of documents ready to go. Mrs. Schwartz was nervous about her husband's going, however. I assured her that for practical political reasons it was unlikely that the House would take action against Dr. Schwartz for delivering the documents to a United States Senator. As quickly as possible we carried the heavy trunk and boxes to my car. At the Mayflower Hotel, we hired a porter to wheel them on a baggage cart to the apartment of Senator Williams. While we were at the Williams apartment, Dr. Schwartz received an urgent telephone call from his wife. He took it in private in another room. Mrs. Schwartz said she had been called by a reporter who told her that since Senator Williams was a Republican, he would probably turn the documents over to Sherman Adams at the White House. The fear was groundless, but Mrs. Schwartz was frantic and made her husband promise to leave the Williams apartment and take the documents with him.

Dr. Schwartz returned to the room and told the Senator it had been suggested that the documents might be taken to Senator Wayne Morse, the Oregon Democrat. We excused ourselves to go telephone Senator Morse and left Senator Williams alone with the documents. I made the call. As I was certain he would—for I had previously talked with him about the regulatory agency scandals—Morse assured me he was interested in reviewing any documents Schwartz had available.

When we arrived at his apartment, Senator Morse greeted us calmly and assured us that he wanted the documents because of his official interest in the regulatory agencies, and we left them with him. Now we felt certain we had created a situation in which it would be virtually impossible for the House to avoid going forward with the investigation. The word would move fast that the files had been examined by a leading Democratic Senator and a leading Republican Senator. It would create a good many complex problems for any House members inclined to ignore or hide the evidence and leads that Schwartz had accumulated.

Before the Schwartz files were returned to the House subcommittee, Senator Morse read them. It was reported to me that most, if not all, of the documents were photographed before they were sent on to Representative Oren Harris, the Arkansas Democrat who was chairman of the House Committee on Interstate and Foreign Commerce.

Until now it appeared Sherman Adams had erected a total shield from investigations by Congress. He had used "executive privilege" to avoid testimony in the Dixon-Yates case. He had been able to make his contacts at the Securities and Exchange Commission without undergoing questioning by the investigating subcommittee which was examining why the SEC had postponed a hearing on Dixon-Yates at a crucial point.

It was Sherman Adams who scribbled his initials on papers to indicate he had approved them for President Eisenhower's signature. Sherman Adams was on the telephone daily to United States senators and congressmen on knotty legislative and patronage matters. Sherman Adams ironed out the problems between cabinet officers, and he dipped his hand into virtually every department from the first months of the Eisenhower administration. Always it was understood that Sherman Adams was speaking for President Eisenhower, or was acting for President Eisenhower. Even when he didn't say, "This is what the President wants," it was understood he was speaking for President Eisenhower.

The legend grew that Sherman Adams was cold and clean as New Hampshire granite—a barrier against the corrupting influence of personal and political favoritism. Coming on the heels of the Truman administration, such a reputation was much admired even when it was known that Adams was not well liked. There were countless stories of his undiplomatic, even rude, treatment of Republican political figures who were interested in a return to some good plain political patronage. It all added to the legend that Sherman Adams was one of the finest influences the Eisenhower administration had brought to Washington.

But there were also those stories of the calls that Sherman Adams made on members of the so-called "independent regulatory agencies." One might commend the White House for keeping a firm hand on agencies directly under the control of the White House, but the regulatory agencies were another matter. Politics were supposed to be kept out.

Shortly after the midnight ride with Dr. Schwartz, I came into the possession of copies of two letters from "Sherm" Adams to "Murray" Chotiner, an attorney for North American Airlines. In the letters, "Sherm" had informed "Murray" that he had discussed the North American Airlines case with the acting head of the CAB. It appeared to be a one-party contact with an official of the CAB during the period when a case was being decided. It appeared to be a direct violation of the rules of the CAB if Adams had done what he stated in the letter he had done for Chotiner, a politically influential California lawyer. I wrote my story on the facts available in the secret files of the House subcommittee.

I caught President Eisenhower's eye early in the February 26, 1958, press conference and he recognized me with a trace of reluctance.

"Mr. President," I started. "Sherman Adams has written

a letter in which he states that he went over the details of a pending Civil Aeronautics Board matter with an acting chairman of the CAB.

"It is contended up on Capitol Hill, that this was a violation of a CAB rule which states—it is improper that there be any communication, private communication that is, by any private or public person with a member of the CAB, with the examiners of the CAB, with the staff while the case is pending, except in those matters prescribed by law.

"I wonder if you could tell us whether you felt Mr. Adams was acting within the proper scope of his authority in this particular matter."

President Eisenhower pleaded ignorance of news stories that had been on page one for days:

"Well, again you are bringing up a thing I have not heard of; but I will say this: There is a number of cases that come under the CAB that the White House must act on. Any time that they refer or have anything to do with the foreign routes that CAB has authorized, or refused to authorize, then the President himself is required to make the final judgment."

The President was confused. He was assuming that the case was a foreign airline route case to which normal rules do not apply. The case about which Adams had written the letter, however, involved a domestic airline, North American Airlines.

"And, very naturally," President Eisenhower continued, "my staff would want to get any additional information that I need. So, I would assume it is so on that case."

"Mr. President," I broke in to explain that the North American case was not a foreign line, but was a domestic airline. "On that line—"

I was cut off by the President's cold stare, and abrupt comment: "I don't want anything more about that."

There was no opportunity to ask another question, but the

record was much clearer to the nation's editorial writers and cartoonists than it was to President Eisenhower.

"Whether the President wants it or not, there ought to be 'more about that' at the very next news conference," commented the St. Louis *Post Dispatch* in a hard-hitting editorial. The editorial pointed out that in the face of rules that would make Adams' contacts "improper," President Eisenhower had "not only evaded a direct question about whether Mr. Adams' intercession was improper but having evaded it, told Reporter Mollenhoff: 'I don't want anything more about that.'"

The Washington *Post* commented that President Eisenhower's answer "gave a damning indictment of his own unfamiliarity with important national affairs yesterday in his fuzzy comments on the relationship of Sherman Adams to the Civil Aeronautics Board.

"For days there have been stories about the accusation by Dr. Bernard Schwartz that Mr. Adams in 1953 discussed the status of North American Airlines with the acting chairman of the CAB on behalf of the airlines counsel, Murray Chotiner. Yet Mr. Eisenhower said, almost incredibly, that he had never heard of the matter."

The *Post* editorial concluded:

"Is it that Mr. Eisenhower just isn't interested, or is it that Mr. Adams, who attempts to ease the Chief Executive's burdens, filters what the President reads?"

Reports were already circulating in Washington that Sherman Adams had made some contacts at two other regulatory agencies on behalf of Bernard Goldfine, a wealthy New England industrialist. However, the claim of "executive privilege" still spread its protective covering over Sherman Adams and others at the White House. The officials of the regulatory agencies continued to refuse to give testimony on contacts with the White House. And, of course, at that stage Sherman Adams had no intention of giving public testimony.

Then, suddenly, the House investigation became a hot issue. Evidence was developed that Richard A. Mack, a member of the FCC, had been involved in some rather complicated financial dealings with a Miami attorney, Thurman A. Whiteside. Whiteside had loaned him money, and there was also an arrangement through an insurance firm which was putting a little extra money in Mack's pocket. Whiteside checks totaling $2650 were received by Mack while he was on the FCC, and Whiteside also gave him a one-sixth interest in an insurance company that sold $20,000 worth of insurance to one of the applicants in the FCC case involving Miami Channel 10.

This case was to lead to the indictment of Mack and Whiteside for alleged conspiracy to fix the award by FCC on Miami Channel 10. Mack was forced to resign from the FCC after a pathetic appearance before the House Legislative Oversight Subcommittee.

In the criminal trial, Mack admitted receiving financial help and "loans" from Whiteside, but contended that it had nothing to do with the award of Channel 10 in Miami to Public Service Television, Inc. Mack contended it was merely an extension of the favors Whiteside had given him since they were boyhood friends. The first trial ended in a hung jury.

The former FCC member never went to trial again. In court he was described as ill and alcoholic, and unable to stand the ordeal of a trial.

Whiteside was tried a second time, and was acquitted on the criminal charge. A short time later, in May 1961, Whiteside was found dead in his Miami office. Death was caused by a self-inflicted bullet wound.

The FCC in a later ruling ordered Public Service Television to stop using Channel 10. The FCC had concluded that the activities of Mack, Whiteside, and others constituted improper conduct in connection with the application of Public Service Television.

The United States Court of Appeals upheld the FCC ruling that Public Service and two other applicants had disqualified themselves by improper practices. The Supreme Court refused to hear an appeal.

Dr. Schwartz and his investigators had pinned down the essential details on the Mack case before Schwartz was fired, and the hearings demonstrated fully the type of activity that at least one of the regulatory agencies had concealed with the claim of "executive privilege." By this time, it was clear to everyone that there were a good many things wrong with the operations of the "big six" regulatory agencies. There was no proof that they were filled with corruption, but there was adequate evidence of a widespread laxity that needed to be examined and exposed.

There had been only the rumors of the Adams-Goldfine relationship while Dr. Schwartz was with the House subcommittee, but once the hearings on Mack were moving, the whole subject of one-party contacts with regulatory agencies came in for closer scrutiny.

Reports that Adams had received a vicuña coat and a $2400 oriental rug from Goldfine evoked interest in Goldfine. These reports were followed by the revelation that Goldfine had lavishly entertained Adams at hotels in New York and Boston, and during the same period of time Adams had made inquiries for Goldfine at the SEC and FTC.

Sherman Adams whipped out a letter which he believed would still the outcry against him. It was a vague letter that simply admitted he had contacted the Federal Trade Commission and the Securities and Exchange Commission on some of Goldfine's problems. However, Adams said he had requested no favors for his friend Goldfine, but ignored the fact that any call from Sherman Adams would flag a case for special attention. The benefits known to have been received by Adams were small, but his relationship with the notorious Goldfine was to become a source of continued embarrassment to the White House. The embarrassment finally forced Adams out of the White House into the open arena of congressional questioners.

Adams went before the House Legislative Oversight Subcommittee in the crowded House Caucus Room. It was his first time to give testimony, and he hoped that it would stop the criticism. President Eisenhower admitted that Adams had been "imprudent" in his relationship with Goldfine. But, the President said, "I need him."

Now nothing could stop the criticism, public and private. It seemed that every week brought more and more revelations of the questionable activities of Bernard Goldfine. There were charges of mislabeling of woolen goods filed by the FTC, and records showed Goldfine firms involved in a long series of mislabeling incidents. Goldfine had not filed proper reports with the SEC for several years. Also, Goldfine had refused to testify on a mysterious $700,000 in cashier's and treasurer's checks he had taken out of his businesses.

Hailed before the committee, Goldfine took the Fifth Amendment, claiming that to answer the questions might tend to incriminate him. Every day that Bernard Goldfine was on the witness stand or otherwise in the public eye was pure misery for the Republican political party. It was apparent that the Republicans would be saddled with Goldfine as long as Sherman Adams remained the number one assistant to President Eisenhower.

And so, on September 22, 1958, Sherman Adams resigned. In a nationwide television broadcast, he said he had "done no wrong" but was the victim of "a campaign of vilification."

Only five days later, a federal grand jury in the District of Columbia returned the indictment charging Richard Mack, the former FCC commissioner, with conspiracy to defraud the government. The indictment charged that Thurman A. Whiteside, a Miami lawyer, had bought Mack's vote in connection with the award of Miami television Channel 10.

Some people paid a heavy price for what had once seemed to them to be clever secretive manipulations to influence governmental decisions. Whiteside crumpled under the strain and died by his own hand. Mack cringed before the court with a plea that he was too ill and too alcoholic to stand trial.

Even a million-dollar fortune couldn't save Bernard Goldfine from the disgrace of a federal prison term. He hired the most expensive lawyers and engaged in every conceivable maneuver to stay out of prison, but in the end lost his freedom and his "friends." He went to prison on a criminal charge of evading more than $800,000 in federal taxes. Although he had boasted bravely that he would not co-operate with the Justice Department in explaining what he did with the missing $800,000, his health broke while in prison and left him a shattered shell of his former self. Later the Internal Revenue Service filed liens against his property totaling more than $7,000,000. The Goldfine magic had turned to mud.

These cases had dramatized the full evil of secret government. The problems of Adams rose directly from the failure of the White House to recognize the dangers involved. It was not necessary to read evil intent into the origin of the blanket secrecy. It was bad enough that the Administration had so self-satisfiedly assumed that things were being handled efficiently and properly and that the press and the Congress were better off kept in the dark where they couldn't stir up trouble.

CHAPTER XII

Ike's Lawyer and the Law

William Pierce Rogers was nominated to be United States Attorney General in the fall of 1957. He had served as Deputy Attorney General under Herbert Brownell from the time the Eisenhower administration came to power in January 1953. When he was nominated for the top post, he was forty-five years old and had been included by President Eisenhower on a select list of bright young Republicans qualified as presidential or vice presidential timber for 1960. He was regarded as the closest friend of Vice President Richard Nixon.

The Senate Judiciary Committee hearing on the Rogers nomination had barely started on January 22, 1958, when Senator Estes Kefauver raised the question of the Eisenhower administration's broad use of "executive privilege."

"Mr. Rogers," the Tennessee Senator said, "many of us in the Senate and in the House have been increasingly alarmed over the expansion of the pleading of privilege on information which congressional committees desire, and feel they have a right to have."

Senator Kefauver explained the philosophy behind the need for full information in a democracy, and then moved to the specific problem:

"I think we all appreciate the fact that under the precedent that when the President has matters up with his Cabinet that he wants to withhold them from public inspection, he has that right; but we find here on numerous occasions when the arms of Congress—the Securities and Exchange Commission, the Federal Communications Commission, the Civil Aeronautics Board, and various and sundry agencies set up by the Congress to administer laws which our Congress has the prime responsibility for administering—they, themselves, are asserting the privilege and they are deciding whether they want to withhold the information or not— things the President does not even know anything about—so that committees of Congress are being hampered in their effort to get information."

Senator Kefauver started to read from a report of the House Government Operations Committee: "The most flagrant abuse of the so-called legal authority is the misuse of the May 17, 1954, letter from the President to the Secretary of Defense at the time of the Army-McCarthy controversy. . . . It seems inconceivable that 19 Government departments and agencies would cite this letter as a shadowy cloak of authority to restrict or withhold information from the Congress and the public. This flimsy pretext of so-called legal authority only serves to demonstrate to what extent executive departments and agencies will go to restrict or withhold information."

Senator Everett Dirksen, the Illinois Republican, interrupted to emphasize that it was a House committee report Senator Kefauver was reading, and that "I want to have that clear."

Senator Kefauver continued: "We had a case here [meaning among Senate committees], where the head of the Securities and Exchange Commission pled privilege to his conversation with Sherman Adams, when apparently Mr. Adams was trying to get a hearing postponed in a quasi-legislative agency.

"We have a report by Senator Olin Johnston's committee in which they take great exception to the pleading of privilege by Mr. [R. W. Scott] McLeod in the Ladejinsky case with which you are familiar. We had the Al Sarena [mining land grant] plea of privilege. We had some pleas of privilege in connection with Mr. Gordon Gray when he was dealing with rapid tax amortization, so it is getting to the point, Mr. Rogers, where not the President but any of these agencies . . . anybody who does not want any information to be made public, just pleads privilege."

Senator Dirksen intervened to volunteer comment "before the Attorney General replies, because I was a part of the proceeding on the McCarthy committee, and I was a part of the proceeding involving the Chairman of the Securities and Exchange Commission."

"If it is all the same to Senator Dirksen, I had rather ask my questions, and you may ask them in your time," Kefauver replied.

"I do not think there has been any great tendency [to secrecy] in the last few years," Rogers said. "I was counsel for committees in . . . 1947, 1948, and 1949 . . . and I do not believe that the problems are much different now and then."

Then Rogers sought to postpone further discussion. "I would like, I think maybe in the interest of time, to delay a full discussion of this, because I have agreed with Senator Hennings to appear before his committee to discuss this whole matter."

Senator Kefauver said he would be glad to see the whole matter examined thoroughly by Senator Hennings, but added: "I do think at this time on such an important matter that you should give us some expression of your position, or what your position will be."

"On the general subject matter," Rogers began, "I believe in the value of congressional investigations. . . . I think they have contributed a great deal to the success of our country, and I think that the executive branch of the Government has the responsibility to make the information available to congressional committees to the fullest extent that it is possible to do so.

"On the other hand," Rogers went on, "I think that the history of the country has indicated that there are exceptions, and that those exceptions have been recognized by each administration throughout history. I do not think that there is any reason why there should be much general disagreement, and I think if we had a chance to discuss those things in detail that probably our views would be pretty much the same."

Senator Kefauver asked Rogers about the use of "executive privilege" by officials of the so-called independent regulatory agencies.

"Well," Rogers said, "I think that possibly there ought to be an even greater attempt made to give all the information to Congress possible, in those agencies. . . . I think you can make mistakes of judgment if you generalize too much on those things, and I think there has been a tendency to do that.

"I remember debating the subject with Russ Wiggins . . . he and Mr. Clark Mollenhoff have been the leaders, and when you get down to it there is not too much in the way of fact. There has been a lot of general observation, but I would like to come up, if you do not mind, and discuss this at length with Senator Hennings' subcommittee."

I knew that Russ Wiggins was well informed on the specific instances of arbitrary withholding. I had tried to discuss a number of specific cases with Rogers but always found him unavailable. Additionally, Senator Hennings had found some difficulty in getting an agreement from Rogers to appear before his Judiciary subcommittee.

"I had not quite understood from your last letter," Senator Hennings told the nominee, "that you were willing to appear before the Constitutional Rights Subcommittee. You did not say that you would not [appear], but I did not quite understand you to say that you would."

Rogers' nomination was confirmed by the Senate, and by the time he appeared before the Hennings subcommittee six weeks later he had become the leading spokesman for the ultimate in secrecy under the claim of "executive privilege." Rogers claimed that the executive branch of the government could properly refuse to give Congress any document that included any advice, recommendation, or conclusion. Although the Constitution says nothing about such a right, Rogers contended that the executive branch did have an "inherent right" to refuse to give testimony or produce records. He further contended that no law of Congress could force production of such records.

This in essence was the position he presented to the Constitutional Rights Subcommittee on March 6, 1958. In addition, smiling, back-patting Bill Rogers now also claimed that the so-called independent regulatory agencies—the FCC, ICC, SEC, CAB, FTC, and FPC—could exercise "executive privilege." Such a position at the nomination hearing might have created serious problems on his confirmation, for at that time the House Legislative Oversight Subcommittee was engaged in the probe of White House and political influence on the regulatory agencies recounted in the foregoing chapter.

At issue when Rogers testified on March 6 was the question of whether the Congress should amend the "Housekeeping Statute" (5 U.S.C. 22) by stating that this statute covering custody of records could not be used as a justification for withholding records from Congress or the public. Rogers opposed the amendment but said that if it passed, it still could not interfere with the broad right he claimed under "executive privilege."

When Representative George Meader, the Michigan Republican, learned of the Rogers testimony he was enraged.

Meader and Rogers had both served as counsel for Senate investigating committees in the late 1940s, and Meader had firsthand knowledge of the investigations that Rogers conducted of the Truman administration. He also knew that Rogers had been sharply critical of secrecy in the Truman administration.

"Curious things seem to happen to individuals when they move from one end of Pennsylvania Avenue to the other," said Representative Meader. He urged the Congress to "strike down" Rogers' claim with legislation declaring specifically that records must be given to Congress. He referred to the "executive privilege" as "nonexistent imagery" which had no support in the Constitution, in the laws, or in the decisions of the federal courts. Throwing aside all political partisanship, Republican Meader told the House that if the Rogers doctrine prevailed the executive will "become the master, not the servant, of the people."

Senator Thomas C. Hennings, whose subcommittee had heard the Rogers testimony, was equally alarmed. A few days after the hearings Hennings received a letter from Rogers designed "to clarify" his testimony. On March 6, Rogers had testified:

"Now I don't recall any instance when Washington, Jefferson or Truman or anyone else ever relied upon this [the Housekeeping Statute] as a basis for 'executive privilege' for withholding information. It is something entirely different. This is a bookkeeping statute which says they keep the records, they hold them physically. It doesn't relate at all to 'executive privilege'."

While stating that the Housekeeping Statute included no right to withhold information, Rogers in the same hearing admitted that it had been erroneously used by officials who had meant to use the "executive privilege" to keep government records secret.

In a letter that followed his testimony, however, Rogers

completely reversed himself and stated that the Housekeeping Statute is "a legislative expression and recognition of the 'executive privilege'."

Hennings replied that Rogers' letter of explanation was "incompatible" with his testimony. He said that Rogers' letter was not only "inconsistent" from a legal standpoint, but "completely baffling when compared with his oral testimony. In almost two years of investigations and study of the subject of freedom of information," Hennings continued, "I have come across a number of cases where various misguided, secrecy-minded executive department officials, eagerly seeking authority to justify withholding information from the Congress and the public have tortured the simple provisions of the [law] . . . beyond all recognition. This interpretation now offered by the Attorney General in his letter surpasses all of these others so far."

On the specific point at issue, Chairman Hennings wrote that he believed the Housekeeping Statute had no connection with constitutional claims of "executive privilege." "I am amazed at the Attorney General's assertion that it does. I think the Attorney General's letter presents overwhelming proof of the urgent need to amend [the law] . . . to make clear beyond any doubt that Congress intended it to be merely a housekeeping statute and not an instrument of censorship."

Rogers' testimony had sent his critics scurrying to the records. When he was chief counsel for a Senate subcommittee investigating a loyalty case in the Truman administration, Rogers had been balked by an executive order issued by President Truman barring Congress from personnel files in loyalty investigations. The records showed that Rogers had fought against this secrecy, limited as it was. The committee report, written under his direction, stated:

"Congress is entitled to know the facts giving rise to the requests and to satisfy itself by firsthand information that the reasons are valid. Any other course blinds the legislative branch and permits action only when the president provides a 'seeing-eye dog' in the form of a request for legislation required by the executive.

"If the subcommittee is denied the right to examine the facts in specific cases where there appears to be a breakdown in the loyalty program, it cannot make a complete appraisal of the program."

I had the switch in Rogers' thinking very much in mind when, less than a month after his appearance, the Hennings subcommittee called me to testify as a representative of the freedom of information committee of the national journalism fraternity, Sigma Delta Chi. I told the subcommittee I opposed any general legislation to allow officials to hide records, and felt that in those areas where secrecy is needed it could be covered by specific legislation.

"We have seen the proof year after year," I testified, "that the unlimited grant of the right to hide the record will lead to abuse of power, corruption and mismanagement.

"Of course, the Attorney General tells us he does not believe that secrecy is being used to hide errors or crimes in the executive branch of Government. Mr. Rogers felt different about this ten years ago. Then he was . . . busy digging out and exposing the crimes, favoritism, and errors which he felt were being covered up by secrecy. . . . We might say that Mr. Rogers was highly successful."

I continued:

"Mr. Rogers may feel things are different today. However, we can never trust the judgment of those in power who might be inclined to make self-serving declarations on their own virtues. This has happened often in the past. We know now that at least eight or ten congressional committees have made it clear they are not as sure as Mr. Rogers that secrecy is not being used to hide crimes, favoritism, and blunders today.

"It is not necessary to arrive at any conclusion on the virtues of this administration or any administration, to conclude that secret government is not in keeping with democracy.

"Even if we accept an administration's declaration on the many virtues it possesses, we must be guided by this principle: 'Never trust a good man to make secret decisions for you, if it would frighten you to lodge the same power in an evil man or a man who is on the other side of the political fence.'"

In the course of my testimony, Senator Roman Hruska, the Nebraska Republican, sought to defend the Eisenhower administration's claim of "executive privilege" in the May 17, 1954, letter:

"He [President Eisenhower] directed that the Secretary of the Army instruct his employees not to disclose information, and the large segment of the American press at that time hailed that decision as being something very fine and very wise and very just."

No one was going to get me to defend those uninformed editorials that had been based on the belief that the May 17, 1954, letter was a single shot of secrecy aimed at Senator McCarthy. I was on much firmer ground when the subject switched to the case of *McGrain v. Daugherty* (1927) in which the Supreme Court stated that the power to compel witnesses to produce records and testify is a necessary part of the legislative function.

"Under the Rogers doctrine, the Congress is reduced to a third-rate division of Government," I said. "Its investigations can be limited to what officials in the executive branch of the Government feel it is wise to produce. If the Government has full discretion as to which facts will be made available to the public, the press, or the Congress, then there is no more than half freedom [to investigate].

"I do not want to be limited in my reporting to the self-serving declaration from men like Richard A. Mack as to what a fine job is being done at the Federal Communications Commission.

"I do not want to be limited to the comments of T. Lamar Caudle, Assistant Attorney General under the Truman administration, as to what a fine job is being done in the prosecution of tax-law violations.

"I do not want to be limited to the comments of Harold Talbott, former Air Force Secretary, as to how he is handling Air Force procurement.

"I do not want to be limited to the statements of former Secretary of Interior Fall that the handling of Teapot Dome oil reserves was really in the public interest."

Also called to testify for Sigma Delta Chi was V. M. (Red) Newton, the managing editor of the Tampa *Tribune*. Herbert Brucker, editor of the Hartford *Courant*, testified on behalf of the American Society of Newspaper Editors. And Harold Cross, the able lawyer for the A.S.N.E., submitted a legal analysis.

Nearly all newspaper, broadcasting, and legal organizations favored the Moss-Hennings amendment to the Housekeeping Statute. It passed Congress with ease despite Administration opposition and on August 12, 1958, President Eisenhower signed it.

The amendment to the Housekeeping Statute said simply: "This section does not authorize the withholding of information from the public or limiting the availability of records to the public." However, as he signed it into law, President Eisenhower said: "It is not intended to, and indeed could not, alter the existing power of the head of an executive department to keep appropriate information or papers confidential in the public interest. The power in the executive branch is inherent under the Constitution."

President Eisenhower had obviously accepted the Rogers theory in full. He had accepted the misleading precedents set out in a Justice Department memorandum in which it was represented to him that George Washington had started all this withholding from Congress. He had been convinced by his subordinates that the "executive privilege" claims made between 1954 and 1958 usurped no more authority than George Washington had. And he had been convinced by some of his advisers that he would be weakening the presidency if he did not stand by the extreme "executive privilege" doctrine.

Robert Donovan, in his book *The Inside Story*, related that President Eisenhower "told the Cabinet he wanted it clearly understood that he was never going to yield to the point where he would become known as a President who had practically crippled the Presidency." This determination accounted for President Eisenhower's frequent use of the comment that he was merely reiterating a principle used by Presidents "back to the time of George Washington."

The "historic precedents," as I have indicated earlier, did not stand up under close investigation. In an article for the Federal Bar *Journal* of January 1959, J. Russell Wiggins, executive editor of the Washington *Post and Times Herald*, told how the historic background—as President Eisenhower understood it—was first described. It appeared in the Federal Bar *Journal* on April 1949, in an article by Herman Wolkinson, a Justice Department lawyer. Wiggins pointed out that an almost identical copy of the Wolkinson memorandum accompanied the May 17, 1954, letter written by Eisenhower to Defense Secretary Wilson. An expanded version of the same material was used by Attorney General Rogers in testimony before Congress.

Wolkinson's article had stated:

"In the great conflicts which have arisen in the administrations of Washington, Jackson, Tyler, Cleveland, Theodore Roosevelt, and Herbert Hoover, the Executive has always prevailed."

Wiggins' painstaking research had convinced him quite otherwise. "This contention is simply not supportable even on the basis of the historical episodes to which Mr. Wolkinson alludes and which the Department of Justice has incorporated in its memorandum."

Getting down to the specific episodes, Wiggins told how Congress, in March 1792, had passed a resolution to initiate an investigation of the disastrous expedition into Indian territory by Major General St. Clair. The investigating committee had asked for all records and papers dealing with the expedition. President Washington did call a cabinet meeting to discuss whether the papers should be given to Congress but finally concluded "to make all the papers available" to Congress. (See Chapter II.)

"If this case is precedent for anything," wrote Wiggins, "it is a precedent to show that the first President was in favor of disclosure, as a principle of government, and as a constitutional matter, except in some possible instances which might later arise, but which in this affair did not exist."

There was one time when President Washington did refuse to send papers to the Hill. This was when the House of Representatives asked him for the instructions and papers furnished our ambassadors in negotiating the Jay treaty. "But," said Wiggins, "this no more sustains the claim to sweeping powers of non-disclosure than the first episode. Here, President George Washington refused the papers on the sound and specific constitutional ground that the Senate and not the House was entrusted with authority to advise and consent on the making of treaties."

After reviewing most of the so-called "withholding precedents" used by Wolkinson and President Eisenhower, Wiggins pointed out that President Jackson and President Tyler had bitterly opposed giving papers to Congress but in the end had forwarded all records requested.

Concluded Wiggins: "In most of Mr. Wolkinson's examples, the Congress prevailed, and got precisely what it sought to get."

Because Senator Hennings and Congressmen Moss and Meader had pushed through the amendment to the House-keeping Statute over Administration objections, they realized that reliance upon "executive privilege" could now become all the more stubborn and Congress would need to take further action.

"In the minds of most people in this country, governmental censorship probably is associated most closely with war or dictatorship," Chairman Hennings said. "Official suppression of the truth generally is regarded as something alien to the American tradition of freedom and incompatible with our system of self-government. Yet, despite these national attitudes, censorship and suppression of the truth are slowly becoming more and more commonplace in our federal government, and secrecy threatens to become the rule rather than the exception."

From the Republican side, the two Democrats were joined by Congressman Meader. "The net effect of the Attorney General's statement," said Meader, "is that the executive branch of the Government will give to the Congress or its committees such information as the executive branch chooses to give and no more. I wonder if the American people and their elected representatives in Congress appreciate the significance of this . . . pronouncement of the executive branch of the Government."

Meader declared that the Rogers doctrine "makes possible a rigged, distorted, slanted" picture of what is going on in a Government agency.

"The unlimited discretion in the executive branch of the Government over access to information in its possession asserted by the Attorney General, would vest in the departments the power by ex parte presentations of half truths to build a record which would permit only one conclusion."

In an analysis that filled six pages in the *Congressional Record,* Meader pointed out that Rogers admitted there was "no judicial precedent governing this question" of "executive privilege." "More study, not less, is required for intelligent policy making in these days," he pleaded. "This asserts a doctrine of executive power which I believe is wholly out of keeping with our concept of democracy and self-government. It smacks of totalitarianism, and I hope it will never prevail in this country."

But the nonpartisan plea for reason and law made little impression. The Eisenhower administration was smug in its popularity. Leaders of Congress were too busy with political chores to pay attention to any problem not connected with the business of getting re-elected. The press could not or would not think logically or consistently on the subject. Secrecy that stood in the way of an individual reporter or newspaper was deplored by that reporter or newspaper, but by too few others. For the most part the attack on secrecy lacked co-ordination, consistency, and enlightened concern.

CHAPTER XIII

Muzzling the Public's Watchdog

Joseph Campbell had been treasurer and vice president of Columbia University while General Dwight D. Eisenhower was president of that institution. A pleasant and friendly relationship developed between the two men, and General Eisenhower was attracted by Campbell's competency in accounting and finance. After General Eisenhower was elected President, he named Campbell a member of the Atomic Energy Commission in 1953.

A year later President Eisenhower named Joseph Campbell Comptroller General of the United States in charge of the General Accounting Office (GAO). It is an important fifteen-year-term office designed to serve the Congress as the "financial watchdog" of all spending in the executive departments and agencies. No single office in the United States is more vital to the task of forcing the sprawling federal government to administer the laws fairly and make expenditures according to the laws.

The GAO was established in the Budgeting and Accounting Act of 1921 as an arm of the legislative branch of government. Once the Comptroller General has been appointed by the President, he becomes an agent of the Congress. To assure the independence of the office, the Congress established the long term and provided that the incumbent could be removed from office only by joint resolution of Congress or by impeachment.

The Budgeting and Accounting Act also gave the GAO the power to examine all information and reports in order to determine whether money was being spent in a legal manner. The section on access to records states:

"All departments and establishments shall furnish to the Comptroller General such information regarding the powers, duties, activities, organization, financial transactions, and methods of business of their respective offices as he may from time to time require of them; and the Comptroller General, or any of his assistants or employees, when duly authorized by him, shall for the purpose of securing such information, have access to and the right to examine any books, documents, papers, or records of any such department or establishment."

The law allowed but one exception to the Comptroller General's legal right to demand and obtain access to "records of any such department or establishment." That one exception gave the Secretary of State the power to determine whether there should be a publication of expenditures of funds used in dealings or treaty making with foreign nations.

The law should have been clear to anyone. The GAO auditors were to be given access to all papers and all records dealing with the expenditure of federal funds. It was the only way they could carefully examine contracts and determine whether any frauds or illegal procedures were involved.

But through the years, as might be expected in a bureaucracy, some officials had been reluctant to put all the cards on the table for the GAO. The reluctance increased in proportion to the bungling, mismanagement, or fraud that might be uncovered by prying GAO investigators.

In the first years of Joseph Campbell's tenure as Comptroller General, his office faced some of the normal bureaucratic reluctance. But, on the whole, the holding back was spotty. Usually the departments produced the records demanded when the inspection provisions of the Budgeting and Accounting Act were pointed out to them.

By 1958, however, the use of "executive privilege" had become so widespread that it was interfering with the work of the GAO. The interference gradually came to light through the work of an Armed Services subcommittee headed by Representative F. Edward Hebert, the Louisiana Democrat. Chairman Hebert had asked Comptroller General Campbell to do a thorough study of the multibillion-dollar Air Force ballistic missile program. He had also set the GAO on the trail of a dozen other smaller projects where it appeared that influence, favoritism, incompetence, or fraud had cost the taxpayers millions of dollars in excess costs.

To Chairman Hebert this unjustified secrecy was serious business. For nearly ten years he had been engaged in important investigations which had proved that the military services could not be relied upon to police their own spending. It was vital that there be an adequate policing job on a Defense budget that totaled about 40 billion dollars a year —approximately half of the entire federal budget. Year after year, Chairman Hebert and Chief Counsel John Courtney had conducted hearings showing incredible waste and inefficiency. The staff of the Hebert subcommittee was small, and Chairman Hebert was forced to rely on the GAO for the major part of the auditing work and legal studies.

The Defense Department could not avail itself of the claim of "national security" when the GAO auditors started an investigation because the GAO auditors were cleared to handle "Secret" and "Top Secret" classified material in the same manner that Defense officials were. Lacking the "national security" claim, the military services latched onto the claim of "executive privilege." One directive followed another, gradually pulling down the secrecy curtain. The periodic, quiet protests by Campbell went unnoticed by the

public until the usually mild-mannered Comptroller General
fired off a letter to Defense Secretary Neil McElroy.

"These restrictions," Campbell wrote, "could seriously
hamper the General Accounting office in performing its
statutory responsibility and will impede the performance of
our work."

He pointed out to McElroy that his GAO auditors could
not do their job in the face of directives that prohibited
them from examining the Inspector General reports, and
allowed them only a summary of reports as approved by the
Secretaries of the various armed services.

In a letter to Chairman Hebert, Campbell made his complaint more specific:

"Any information or factual data directly bearing on a
program of activity subject to audit by the General Accounting Office should not be withheld or subjected to procedures
designed to screen official documents, papers, or records,
by the authority or activity being audited."

Later, in a letter to the Moss subcommittee on Government Information, the Comptroller General stated that he
was seeking to make a study of the activity of the Inspector
General of the Air Force to determine how effective the
internal investigations had been.

He stated that to conduct such an investigation, the GAO
inspection must include:

1 A survey of the Air Force procurement methods (advertising versus negotiation).
2 A survey of procurement quantitative and qualitative
   program changes.
3 A survey of contract cost overruns.

"It is essential that such reports be made available to
the General Accounting Office in order that we can evaluate
the effectiveness of the department's system of internal control and to preclude unwarranted and unnecessary duplica-

tion of effort in the internal audit and the independent reviews made by this office," Campbell wrote.

"There is no basis why reports on the subject of the types pointed out above should not be made available to the General Accounting Office unless the purpose is to delay or hamper the efforts of the office to disclose all facts bearing upon the activity or area under audit.

"We believe that any departmental regulation denying to the General Accounting Office access to any report relating to 'internal audit and control' is contrary to the law."

It should be remembered that this was not a Democratic congressman or senator accusing a Republican administration. This was Joseph Campbell, long-time friend of President Eisenhower, charging that the Eisenhower administration was acting "contrary to the law" in the claim of an "executive privilege."

Congressman John Moss subsequently declared that President Eisenhower was not discharging his duties under the Constitution. Under Article II, Section 3 of the Constitution, the President is obliged to "take care that the laws be faithfully executed . . ." In this instance, President Eisenhower was not only disregarding the Budgeting and Accounting Act but also supporting those acting "contrary to the law," Moss said.

Although the fuss had started over GAO access to a sixty-two-page Air Force inspector general report on the ballistic missile program (see Appendix C), the real issue was whether the Air Force, the Army, the Navy, or any other executive agency could arbitrarily refuse to give reports, papers, and financial records to the GAO.

It was difficult to follow President Eisenhower's thinking. This was a period of time when President Eisenhower and members of his administration were emphasizing that financial problems could be one of the nation's big worries. One of the major problems, they believed, was making sure the government was getting its money's worth from military spending.

Even in times past, when GAO investigators were given maximum access to records, serious scandals had been unearthed. Most of them were not discovered by the military establishment but came to light only after the GAO or the congressional committees went to work. Chairman Hebert and Campbell had a long record of fruitful hearings to back them in questioning the wisdom (to say nothing of the legality) of allowing our military spenders to erect more barriers for the GAO auditors—the only independent outside check on the billions spent on military matters.

At the presidential press conference on November 5, 1958, I raised the question of the right of the General Accounting Office to examine reports of the Air Force and the Defense Department.

"Mr. President," I said, "you have mentioned the spending in the Defense Department here as one of the important issues, and the General Accounting Office, which is the watchdog on frauds and extravagances in the various agencies, has been barred from reports over in the Air Force and the Defense Department generally, and on this they [the Air Force and Defense Department officials] claim that they have authority from you to withhold reports if it is 'expedient to do so.'"

I tried to make the question conform as much as possible to the precise trouble area between the GAO and the Defense Department.

"I wonder," I continued, "if you have given that authority [to withhold] and if you feel that the GAO should have a full rein to go in and investigate all indications of fraud and extravagance?"

Replied the President: "You are obviously talking about some special thing that I would have to study before I could make—give an answer. I have stated this time and time again: I believe that every investigating committee of the Congress, every auditing office, like the GAO, should always have the opportunity to see official records if the security of our country is not involved."

President Eisenhower was now saying that the GAO should have all records unless the security of our country was involved. I tried to pin him down on it.

"Will they claim this, Mr. President, under 'executive privilege—'" I started my question.

President Eisenhower cut in before I had finished to avoid any further comment. "No, that's all I have to say—I told you that is all I had to say for the moment."

Representative Clare Hoffman, the wily Michigan Republican, noted that President Eisenhower's answer seemed to bar use of "executive privilege" in refusing reports to the GAO. A few days after the press conference, he wrote President Eisenhower to call attention to the press conference exchange and to ask:

"Did you mean to imply by your comments that the complete text of Inspector General reports, including recommendations, be made available to Congress and the General Accounting Office?"

President Eisenhower's letter to Representative Hoffman on the same day again barred the GAO from the full reports of inspectors general. The President said that "facts" in the reports would be made available to the GAO, but that "recommendations and other advisory matter" were not to be released (see Appendix C).

The whole situation landed right back where it had started. The Air Force, Navy, or Army officials would still screen the Inspector General reports, eliminate material they didn't want to fall into the hands of GAO auditors, and pass out their own self-serving summary to the investigators. Law and logic had fallen by the wayside. The Budgeting and Accounting Act might as well not have been written for all the good it was doing in forcing departments to produce all pertinent documents.

The next big test came with the Navy. In February 1959, Comptroller General Campbell wrote to the Moss subcommittee stating that the secrecy curtain made it impossible for him to fulfill his responsibility to audit Navy financial affairs.

"We consider it illogical, impractical and contrary to express provisions of the law for public officials to withhold, in their discretion, information concerning the discharge of their public trust," Campbell wrote.

"We are advising the Secretary of Defense and the Secretary of the Navy that we are unable to properly discharge our statutory responsibility if information needed in our work is denied to our representatives in the performance of our audits."

Representative William L. Dawson, chairman of the parent House Government Operation Committee, instructed Moss to prepare for public hearings. He wrote Campbell:

"I am sure everything possible will be done to overcome the repeated arrogance of Federal executive officials whose denial of information to the General Accounting Office flouts the clear law of the land."

Comptroller General Campbell said that the "executive privilege" claim was being made by the Secretary of the Navy on grounds that "he believes full disclosure of rank opinions, advice and recommendations from persons at lower levels . . . would not be in the public interest.

"This same reasoning is now being applied by the various bureaus and offices in the day-to-day work of their employees.

"We believe that sound management practices require that observations, opinions, and recommendations by subordinates and any other matters considered in making a decision should be a matter of record.

"All of these are matters upon which judgments are founded and subsequent decision and actions are based. Such documentation serves as a protection to the individual making the decisions or taking the action as well as furnishing a sound basis for subsequent appraisal of their timeliness, effectiveness and honesty."

Campbell complained that under Navy procedure at that time "the individuals having custody of the materials are required to screen the material and remove from the official files any data they or their superiors feel we should not have.

"These actions provide a means by which the Department could conceal substantive evidence of waste, extravagance, improvident management, poor procurement practices, or other adverse conditions."

By March of 1959, Campbell had full proof that he could not rely on the summary reports submitted to him by the Navy. He declared that the Navy had submitted two reports on one subject that were "incorrect representations" of the government's action. "The second version of the report, while containing twice as many pages, is also incomplete and inadequate because of the use of self-exercised censorship."

Campbell said that the secrecy was not only illegal and bad government but that it was mighty expensive. He explained that the secrecy deprived the GAO auditors of information already accumulated at the taxpayers' expense. This meant that the GAO was forced to go out and duplicate work already done if it was to make any effort to fulfill its responsibility.

Comptroller General Campbell put no price tag on the extra cost for a GAO audit of the Navy. However, the GAO did estimate that lack of access to the Air Force Inspector General reports made that audit cost at least $125,000 more than necessary. Though the cost of the audit could have been avoided with the proper co-operation of the Air Force, the audit ultimately disclosed millions of dollars in bungling and waste in the Air Force missile program—all covered up in the name of "executive privilege."

The Richmond *Times-Dispatch* commented:

"The amazing thing about this situation is that President Eisenhower backs the armed services in withholding vital information from the GAO. He has been told by his legal advisers that 'executive privilege' has some validity, where it is in essence nothing but the determination of bureaucrats to keep the GAO from seeing their books.

"This bogus doctrine forced the GAO to spend an extra $125,000 in making its inquiry into Air Force mismanagement. . . . Just how much longer is the public going to put up with this sort of thing?"

I knew that Virginius Dabney, editor of the Richmond *Times-Dispatch*, was fed up with this expensive and undemocratic secrecy. So was J. Russell Wiggins, executive editor of the Washington *Post and Times Herald*; James Pope, executive editor of the Louisville *Courier-Journal*; Herbert Brucker, editor of the Hartford *Courant*; V. M. (Red) Newton, managing editor of the Tampa *Tribune*; and Harold Cross, the special counsel for the American Society of Newspaper Editors.

The Chicago *Daily News*, the St. Louis *Post-Dispatch*, and *The Wall Street Journal* were among the other top papers firmly opposed to the secrecy cover-up. But despite several excellent editorials, the problem just wasn't flamboyant enough to catch the attention of the public or even most reporters. Too many news stories and editorials in other papers merely repeated the self-serving justifications of the Eisenhower administration without determining whether the assertions were true.

CHAPTER XIV

Hiding the Laos Mess

By the summer of 1959, Representative Porter Hardy was fed up with arbitrary executive secrecy. The lanky Virginia Democrat was getting a double dose of "executive privilege" and had nearly reached the end of his patience. He was a member of the Armed Services subcommittee headed by Chairman Edward Hebert, and therefore had firsthand knowledge of how the Defense Department was hampering investigations of military waste.

Representative Hardy was also chairman of his own Foreign Operations and Monetary Affairs Subcommittee. This subcommittee (of the House Government Operations Committee) was responsible for investigating the handling of more than 60 billion dollars in foreign aid by the State Department and the International Cooperation Administration (ICA).

The Hardy subcommittee had a small staff of a half dozen headed by John T. Reddan, the chief counsel. Under the best circumstances, Hardy knew that they would be able to look into only a few reports of mismanagement or fraud. But a little scrutiny should soon tell whether the internal investigations of ICA were being conducted in such a manner that the Congress could rely on ICA to police itself.

To find out how well ICA was performing, it was necessary to examine the files of complaints of fraud or mismanagement and to determine how these complaints were being followed up by ICA investigators. But the ICA barred Hardy's committee staff members from examining the investigation files as well as the evaluation reports ICA was making on its own operations. Such files, Chairman Hardy was told, would contain "advice, recommendations and conclusions," and, according to President Eisenhower's May 17, 1954, letter, therefore, could not be released.

The investigation proceeded nonetheless. It was slow work, but with patience and persistence Chief Counsel Reddan, Counsel Richard Bray, Jr., Counsel Miles Q. Romney, and Investigator Walton Woods pieced together the information ICA had denied them. They got it by interviewing former government employees, examining the files of business firms with government contracts, and taking trips to other lands to personally examine foreign-aid spending.

The little country of Laos in southeast Asia was one of the first on which they concentrated. The picture was not pretty. The administration of U.S. aid was creating at least as many problems as it was trying to solve.

The aid program in Laos started in January 1955, when that nation was granted its full independence. Laos had been a part of French Indochina with Cambodia and Vietnam. Independence for Laos had meant that the United States took over the support of its entire military budget—41 million dollars in 1955, 47 million dollars in 1956, 43 million dollars in 1957, and 30 million dollars in 1958. Most of it went to support a 25,000-man army. The subcommittee later concluded that this military aid plus about 1.5 million dollars annually in economic assistance added up to the fact that the United States was "virtually supporting the entire economy."

As early as June 1957, the subcommittee received reports indicating the foreign-aid program in Laos was being damaged by waste, inefficiency, and poor judgment. After preliminary inquiries, the formal investigation was started on April 10, 1958.

The requests for ICA files on Laos foreign-aid spending were rejected by ICA Director James W. Riddleberger. The ICA also barred Chairman Hardy from files on India, Bolivia, Brazil, and Guatemala.

A few months later, the ICA refused to let the GAO auditors see the files on Laos.

Chairman Hardy was irked with the frustration, but downright furious at what he considered to be a disregard of the law. Certainly the ICA reports on Laos should be made available to the GAO, for the Budgeting and Accounting Act of 1921 provided explicitly that all records of all departments must be made available to the GAO auditors.

Furthermore, when the foreign-aid program had been established in 1948, the debates had included discussion of the accounting on foreign aid and the necessity for availability of information to Congress.

At that time Senator Arthur Vandenberg, the Michigan Republican, commented:

"There are several points in the bill where it is provided that Congress is to be advised. In addition, we are creating . . . the 'watchdog' committee [Joint Committee on Economic Cooperation] . . . which will be entitled to all information of every character at all times."

Despite the law and the intention of the lawmakers, the ICA had clamped the secrecy lid on, and kept it on. ICA also rejected GAO requests for information on foreign-aid spending in Formosa, India, Vietnam, Pakistan, France, Turkey, and others.

In its investigation of but one of the foreign-aid programs—the one in Laos—the Hardy subcommittee unearthed enough evidence of incompetence, laxity, mismanagement, and fraud to fill scores of pages of an official report.

The military program for a 25,000-man Laotian army, for

example, arose from a political decision made by the State Department and contrary to the recommendations of the Joint Chiefs of Staff and the Defense Department. "Significant military opinion has suggested a force of 12,000 to 15,000," the Hardy subcommittee reported.

The subcommittee also found favoritism, conflict of interest, and bribery in connection with ICA contracts in Laos. "Edward T. McNamara, [ICA] public works and industry officer, accepted bribes totaling at least $13,000 from Willis H. Bird and Gerald A. Peabody of the Universal Construction Co., in return for helping them secure lucrative contracts and overlooking deficiencies in their performance."

The subcommittee reported dozens of incidents of minor officials' showing favoritism toward firms that later employed them. One sharp charge was aimed at the man who headed the United States Operations Mission (USOM) during part of this period.

"Carter dePaul, former USOM director, sold his 1947 Cadillac upon his departure from Laos to Gerald A. Peabody, head of Universal, at an inflated price [about $3000]. Uncontroverted evidence indicates the vehicle was at that time inoperable, and that shortly thereafter it was cut up and the pieces dropped down an abandoned well. In the interim, it had stood rusting in front of Universal's main office, where it was the subject of scornful amusement by Laotians and Americans alike."

More shocking than the frauds was the evidence dug up by the subcommittee showing that U. S. Embassy officials in Laos and high ICA officials in Washington took no effective remedial action after receiving reports of corruption and mismanagement. Greater energy was obviously being expended in hiding the mess from Chairman Hardy and his investigators.

The subcommittee's evidence indicated that an investigator for the ICA Auditor Haynes Miller, "was 'railroaded' out of Laos because he was close to discovering the truth about Universal, its bribes, its virtual monopoly of U.S. aid construction projects . . . and its woefully inadequate performance."

This action to remove Auditor Miller seemed more reprehensible to me than any ordinary theft or misuse of money or government power. This was evidence that there was a brutal conspiracy within the U. S. Embassy in Laos to eliminate those officials who were complaining of fraud and mismanagement and to shield persons who were engaged in wrongdoing. It demonstrated what could happen when government officials feel they have an "executive privilege" to hide the records on their activities.

Miller's reports and his persistent efforts to get something done about deficiencies in the program only resulted in his removal. He was "unable to adjust" to Laos, some of his superiors and associates said. U. S. Ambassador J. Graham Parsons sent a telegram to Washington stating he had invited the investigator to resign "because of obvious signs of nervous disorder."

"Ambassador Parsons' opinion of Miller's 'nervous disorder' was rendered without benefit of medical advice," the Hardy subcommittee reported. "This is contrary to Department of State regulations. Competent medical advice was available to the Ambassador and could have been solicited."

"One month later, on October 30, 1957," the report added, "Miller was subjected to a full medical examination in Washington and certified as 'qualified for general duty.'"

Officials of the ICA excused the deficiencies and maladministration in the Laos program with the claim that the aid program, no matter how poorly administered, had saved Laos from Communism.

"This assertion is purely speculative, and can be neither proved nor disproved," the Hardy subcommittee stated in 1959. That was two years before it was generally realized that a corrupt aid program had probably helped the Communists in Laos.

Even in 1959 the Hardy subcommittee concluded "that a lesser sum of money more efficiently administered would have been far more effective in achieving economic and political stability in Laos, and in increasing its capacity to reject Communist military aggression or political subversion."

At a press conference on July 2, 1959, two weeks after the Laos report was issued, William McGaffin, of the Chicago *Daily News*, put the problem of secrecy in ICA to President Eisenhower.

"Mr. President," McGaffin started, "do you see any solution to the quarrel between Congress and the executive branch of the Government over the question of freedom of information?"

"Well, I don't know exactly what you are adverting to when you say freedom of information," President Eisenhower said and then jumped for the safety of George Washington's shadow:

"This question, from the time of Washington, has been a live one. When the Executive determines that something is to the—will damage the security of the United States or its vital interest, then it withholds information that possibly could be put out. But I don't know of any specific thing which you are talking about at this moment."

McGaffin bounced back:

"Mr. President, if I could just spell it out briefly: Congress seems perturbed over various instances where they feel that the executive branch has misused the claim of 'executive privileges' and denied them information which they should have.

"For instance," McGaffin continued: "There are evaluation reports made by the ICA on certain countries which have received mutual security—Formosa, Laos, Brazil, Guatemala—a whole string of them, and Congress has raised the point where they are going to try to pass a law which would compel ICA to turn that information over to them."

President Eisenhower confused the problem with national security in answering:

"Well, there are certain things, particularly in the security field, that, if you reveal, are very obviously damaging to the United States and I think anyone of good sense will see that. And you simply must take measures to see that those things are not revealed.

"And, now, this has been—there is nothing new about this. The Executive, and there seems to be a sort of congenital built-in mutual opposition that I don't know why it occurs, I don't particularly feel it personally, but I know it's there and at times it comes to my attention in one form or another.

"But," said the President, retreating to the safety of his reputation as an honest man, "I am using my own conscience on the matter and when such things as these come to me for decision, I shall continue to do so."

It was a most unsatisfactory answer on a most important question involving the policing of spending by the Defense Department and the ICA. I decided to follow up where the Hardy subcommittee and Bill McGaffin left off. At the next press conference, on July 15, 1959, I caught President Eisenhower's eye.

"Mr. President," I started. "Several committees of Congress have charged that departments of your administration have used the secrecy of the so-called 'executive privilege' to hide imprudence, mismanagement, fraud, and in some cases material which has later resulted in indictments. I wonder if you have taken any steps to correct this?"

President Eisenhower's eyes blazed with anger. Despite his emotion he remained controlled enough to avoid the kind of comments on facts or law that had put him in so much trouble in the past. He said:

"I think you had better put that question in written form and let me take a look at it because you start off, right off the bat, with the premise or implication that someone is guilty of fraud and I don't believe it."

When I attempted to reply that the charges of fraud and mismanagement were included in official reports of Congress, he cut me off sharply. "I will see your letter if you would like to submit it."

In the letter to President Eisenhower, I tried to be careful and to be respectful of his position:

My dear Mr. President: In response to your request, I am submitting the basic question which I asked at the July 15, 1959, press conference. I regret that the statement of the question at the press conference raised any implication of fraud, or knowledge of fraud, at the White House level. Such an implication was not intended. The question was based on the findings of various committees of the Congress. In general the reports dealt with subordinate officials who, it is contended, used the so-called executive privilege in an effort to conceal their activities from investigators of Congress and the General Accounting Office.

Several committees of Congress have made reports charging that officials in some departments of Government have used the secrecy of executive privilege to hide what the committees called carelessness, mismanagement, fraud, and other alleged improprieties. Comptroller General Joseph Campbell has told the Congress that some executive departments have violated the law—the Budgeting and Accounting Act—in withholding reports from him in connection with waste, mismanagement and improprieties. Mr. Campbell has testified before the House Appropriations Committee that this secrecy is a violation of the law, and he also stated that it "could be almost fatal" to vital auditing functions his office performs.

Comptroller General Campbell and the Moss subcommittee, among others, have raised the question as to whether this withholding of information is inconsistent with the Constitutional requirements that the Chief Executive "take care that the laws be faithfully executed."

There is no problem of national security involved. The Air Force and Navy have informed Congress and the GAO that no national security is involved, since the GAO auditors have the same clearance to examine classified material as do the officials in the departments.

Against this background, I would rephrase my question as follows: In the light of the provisions of the Budgeting and Accounting Act, do you feel you have an executive responsibility to carry out the law in line with the Comptroller General's views?

The answer, from Gerald D. Morgan, Deputy Assistant to the President, reached me a few days later on July 21. Morgan merely quoted from the President's letter to Representative Hoffman of some months before, and from other earlier statements of his on "executive privilege."

Morgan wrote, "The President's position has not changed." I was not convinced that President Eisenhower knew what his position was. The letter left all basic questions unanswered.

The foreign-aid bill, amending the Mutual Security Act of 1954, was now before the Congress, and Representative Hardy had tacked on an amendment specifically stating that "all documents, papers, communications, audits, reviews, findings, recommendation reports and other material which relate to the operation or activities of the International Cooperation Administration shall be furnished to the General Accounting Office" and authorized committees of Congress.

On July 24, 1959, President Eisenhower signed the bill with Hardy's amendment, including three provisions for disclosure of information to the Congress or the GAO. In sign-

ing it, however, the President served notice he would not
abide by the disclosure sections:

"I have signed this bill on the express premise that the
three amendments relating to disclosure are not intended to
alter and cannot alter the recognized constitutional duty
and power of the executive with respect to the disclosure
of information, documents, and other materials. Indeed, any
other construction of these amendments would raise grave
constitutional question under the historic separation of
powers doctrine."

Five days later at the July 29, 1959, press conference I
asked the President if he considered the provisions in the bill
to cut off funds to balky agencies to be "a criticism of the
administration's secrecy policies."

President Eisenhower turned red in the face at the reference to "secrecy" in his administration. "You start your
question with an implied fact that is not a fact," he said.
"You say the administration's secrecy policies. There has
been no administration . . ."

I tried to amplify my question, but was cut off.

"Please sit down," the President said sharply. I sat on
orders from the Commander in Chief, and he continued:

"There has been no administration since my memory, and
I have been in this city since 1926, who has gone to such
lengths to make information available as long as the national
security and the national interest of this country is not
involved."

It was fruitless for me to try to stand up and tell him what
was happening in his administration. So I sat still and took
it. The support that came later from editors over the country
was most gratifying.

V. M. (Red) Newton, Jr., managing editor of the Tampa
Tribune, wrote to President Eisenhower:

"Mr. Mollenhoff's question at the press conference about
your administration's 'secrecy policies' had to do with the

House of Representatives provisions in the foreign aid bill that would force the bureaucracy to give information of this foreign aid to the Congress.

"Both the Congress, which votes the expenditure, and the American people, who pay the tax funds, are entitled to full information."

The Richmond *Times-Dispatch* in an editorial entitled "Does Eisenhower Understand?" commented: "Somebody is going to have to explain to President Eisenhower that the 'executive privilege' dogma, which originated in his first term five years ago, is being perverted into a device for 'covering up' and denying the public the facts concerning the government."

The editorial commented on the "corruption, profiteering and mismanagement in Laos" in the ICA, and the fact that the Teapot Dome scandals would never have been uncovered if such a principle as "executive privilege" had been invoked.

"So it would be advisable for Mr. Eisenhower to look into this 'executive privilege' thing much more carefully than he has done so far. He will find that it carries within itself the seeds of scandal, and offers needless temptation to department heads. It should be abolished."

The Wall Street Journal editorialized on the "Misplaced Anger" of President Eisenhower. It gave President Eisenhower full credit as a "man who believes that public office is a public trust." But the *Journal* in its usual fair but solid way called attention to the entire problem of the GAO's obtaining access to government records so it could fulfill its responsibility.

"If he [the President] were to inquire into the extent of secrecy," said *The Wall Street Journal,* "we have an idea the President would be far more angered at some of his own bureaucrats than at the reporter who brought the secrecy to his attention."

The Hartford *Courant,* edited by Herbert Brucker, carried

an equally fine editorial. Brucker was chairman of the Freedom of Information Committee of the American Society of Newspaper Editors, and was one of a handful of the editors who knew the subject thoroughly.

By this time editors of a couple dozen newspapers had done considerable study on the problem of "executive privilege." Although cognizant of the many problems weighing on President Eisenhower, they felt the time had come for him to make himself aware of the insidious secrecy that was creeping into the federal government under his prestige.

It was a week after this press conference that James W. Riddleberger, Director of the ICA, refused to make evaluation reports available to Congress on the foreign-aid program in Laos and Vietnam.

Now Chairman Hardy saw that a disclosure amendment to the Mutual Security law would not be enough to force the Eisenhower administration to produce records for the GAO and the Congress. The 3.1-billion-dollar foreign-aid appropriations bill was still pending in Congress, and Hardy decided to to try to use an amendment to this purse-string measure to force the Eisenhower administration to produce records.

The House was unanimous in adopting the Hardy amendment to the appropriations bill. This amendment provided that the Comptroller General could shut off aid funds to any program if records were refused to Congress and GAO investigators.

The Eisenhower administration was gravely concerned over this amendment. Riddleberger voiced the opposition, and the Senate weakened in the face of administration pressure. The Senate version of the appropriations bill carried the provision that the President could authorize withholding by a simple certification "that he has forbidden its being furnished . . . and his reason for so doing." In a late night session the Senate-House conference committee accepted the huge loophole in the Senate version of the appropriations bill.

Representative Hardy recognized it immediately as a loophole that could destroy the effectiveness of his amendment. A simple note from the President would override any request by Congress or the GAO.

Would President Eisenhower read the documents necessary to determine for himself whether a certification for withholding was justified? It seemed more likely to his critics that he would sign certifications continuing to bar the GAO and Congress from a thorough examination of the internal workings of the foreign-aid program. Chairman Hardy's fears were justified. It wasn't long before his requests for information were being met with "certification" from President Eisenhower giving only the most general reasons.

The Congress could have done more than it did. It unquestionably had the necessary power, reaffirmed by the Supreme Court as recently as 1957 in the Watkins case. The Court said:

"The power of Congress to conduct investigations is inherent in the legislative process. That power is broad. It encompasses inquiries concerning the administration of existing laws as well as proposed or possibly needed statutes. It includes surveys of defects in our social, economic, or political system for the purpose of enabling the Congress to remedy them. It comprehends probes into departments of the Federal Government to expose corruption, inefficiency and waste."

I was unsuccessful in my efforts to get Speaker Sam Rayburn or Majority Leader Lyndon B. Johnson interested in taking any effective measures to reaffirm the right of Congress to compel production of records for GAO.

Congress did deliver the Eisenhower administration one blow in 1959 in connection with the "executive privilege" issue. That was when President Eisenhower nominated Ad-

miral Lewis Strauss to be Secretary of Commerce. The hearings before the Interstate and Foreign Commerce Committee
started on March 17, and pulled out past the middle of May.
Although a good many personality clashes were involved,
the role that Strauss had played in the Dixon-Yates contract
and his advocacy of extreme "executive privilege" also
figured.

The report favoring the Strauss confirmation stated: "Our
committee spent much time in detail examination of specific
instances in which it is charged that the nominee withheld
or was grudging in giving information to congressional committees. The few instances charged represent a minute per-
centage of the nominee's dealings with the Congress.

"In fact, the nominee showed great diligence in keeping
the Congress informed," concluded the six Republicans and
two Democrats who signed the majority report.

When questioned about the Dixon-Yates contract, Strauss
had said: "I thought it was a good contract and I still do . . .
it would have cost the people a great deal less than the plant
. . . is now going to cost."

Strauss denied that he had used "executive privilege" to
hold out information from Congress in the Dixon-Yates
controversy.

"No information was withheld by me," he said. "No question failed of answer except one which was several times
repeated and to which I respectfully declined response on
ground that to demand conversations had with the President
or members of his personal staff would be in violation of the
constitutional doctrine of separation of powers . . . I testified that the contract with Mississippi Valley Generating
Company had been entered into at the direction of the President and had been terminated at the direction of the President, and that, I submit, should have been sufficient."

Strauss claimed a total right under "executive privilege" to refuse records to Congress, and the seven-member Democratic minority concluded:

"The record . . . indicates such withholding is without basis in law, and that the nominee had no concern for the law in this respect. From the record it is clear that the nominee time after time has resisted furnishing the appropriate committees of the Congress with information needed in order for Congress to properly perform its legislative functions.

"It appears to us from careful attention to the testimony, that Mr. Strauss had withheld or manipulated information to serve policy or personal ends. On the basis of the record, we have grave doubts as to whether or not information furnished by Mr. Strauss, as Secretary of Commerce, would be accurate or complete."

The minority position was to prevail on the Senate floor where the Strauss nomination was defeated.

Senator Mike Monroney, the Oklahoma Democrat, explained his opposition to the Strauss nomination thus:

"Both the people and the press are entitled to expect from the legislative branch of Government the vigilant protection of the people's right to know. For the Senate to seek to give protection in the exercise of its power of confirmation is not only proper, it is obligatory.

"I conceive it to be basic to democratic government that the people and their elected representatives in the Congress, are entitled to receive from the officials of the executive branch, not merely literal truth, but full information, freely given without design to soothe, to confuse or divert."

When the Strauss nomination was defeated in mid-June, I had hopes that the Congress was on the way to recognizing the problem of "executive privilege" for all that it was. But by the end of the year it was apparent that most of the members of Congress had gone back to their little personal problems and had left Moss, Hennings, Hardy, and a few others to wrestle with the big problem of how to obtain an adequate GAO audit of spending that involved more than half the total national budget.

CHAPTER XV

Defiance to the End, Above the Law

From the investigation of the aid program in Laos, Representative Porter Hardy and his subcommittee staff moved on to the aid programs in Latin America. The subcommittee had examined some Latin-American aid programs as early as 1955 and unearthed several deficiencies. But the Eisenhower administration had claimed that the shortcomings were due largely to the newness of the programs and suggested that the subcommittee examine them again five years later.

The five years had now elapsed, and on April 28, 1960, Chairman Hardy notified Secretary of State Christian Herter and ICA Director Riddleberger that he was initiating an investigation of the aid programs to Brazil, Uruguay, Argentina, Chile, Bolivia, Peru, and Colombia.

Several new laws were on the books to facilitate the investigation. The 1959 law establishing the office of Inspector General and Comptroller (OIGC) in the State Department provided that:

"All documents, papers, communications, audits, reviews, findings, recommendations, reports, and other material which relate to the operation or activities of the Office of Inspector General and Comptroller shall be furnished the General Accounting Office and to any committee of the Congress, or any duly authorized subcommittee thereof."

The Congress in 1960 amended the Mutual Security Act providing the GAO could shut off funds to the OIGC if that agency did not furnish records requested in a reasonable time.

Chairman Hardy's staff had also called his attention to another law (5 U.S.C. 105 [a]) which provided that every department shall, upon request of the Government Operations Committee, "furnish any information requested of it relating to any matters within the jurisdiction of said committee."

Added to these laws, and the previously mentioned Budgeting and Accounting Act of 1921, was the fact that the State Department was preparing to ask Congress for more money for aid to Latin America. The stage was legally and psychologically well set for co-operation. And Chairman Hardy was indeed advised that he would receive full co-operation. It never came. When his first requests for files on the Bolivia program produced no results in six weeks, Hardy notified the State Department and ICA that hearings would begin on the information policy on June 28, 1960.

The hearings revealed that the State Department had constructed an involved thirteen-step routine for clearing papers for Congress, and the papers Hardy requested simply had not been cleared. Eric H. Hager, legal adviser of the Department of State, identified himself as the man responsible for the new system.

It was found that in one instance it took six weeks for one subcommittee request to clear eight of the thirteen steps. When Chairman Hardy tried to find out what had happened to the request for documents, he learned that the request and the documents were resting in the "in box" in the Office of the Assistant Secretary of State for Congressional Relations. The papers had been gathering dust in the box for two weeks and were only moved when the State Department started to prepare for the hearing.

In the report on the hearings, Hardy's subcommittee explained the need for original documents as "the best evidence available" on the internal operations of ICA.

"It has been the policy and practice of the subcommittee, in order to insure accurate reporting of these complex operations, to support its findings with documentary corroboration from files of the executive agencies," the report stated.

"The subcommittee has sought to obtain the facts from the documents and records . . . as they are prepared in the ordinary course of doing business, rather than to rely upon oral testimony or upon secondary documents prepared especially for the subcommittee's consideration."

The report scored "executive privilege" as a "nebulous doctrine" that had plagued the subcommittee with delays. Again it was pointed out that the withholding of information was in violation of clear laws imposing a duty to make records available to Congress. The report stated that the subcommittee had sought to be reasonable in its request, and "on several occasions [has] withdrawn its requests for particular documents at the suggestion of the executive branch. Examples of documents in this category are certain memoranda recording high-level discussions between Department of State officials and senior officials of foreign governments."

The report stated it should be understood that this willingness to refrain from pressing for certain documents was not a recognition of any right to withhold them. It continued:

"No court decision has settled the question of whether executive officials may refuse to honor a request of a congressional committee for papers, documents and records. Many court decisions, however, have upheld the power of congressional committees to obtain records and papers in the possession of private individuals, corporations, and associations even though such records might be regarded as of a highly personal nature. It logically follows that the power of Congress to obtain information regarding the public business, the exercise of authority granted by Congress, or the expenditure of funds appropriated by Congress would likewise be upheld in the event of a court test.

"If Congress is to discharge its constitutional legislative and policymaking functions, it must have reliable information about the public business."

To allow the executive branch to pick and choose what the Congress would be allowed to examine "can, and frequently does, result in giving Congress a distorted picture," the report said.

Then it suggested the use of two existing powers of Congress to oppose this abuse of power by the executive: the power of subpoena, and the power of the purse.

"The power of subpoena, however, should be used only as a last resort. Utilizing the power of the purse, the Congress can and should provide, in authorizing and appropriating legislation, that the continued availability of appropriated funds is contingent upon the furnishing of complete and accurate information relating to the expenditure of such funds to the General Accounting Office and to the appropriate committees of Congress at their request."

A week after the report was issued, Chairman Hardy sent a letter to the ICA, State Department, and the Development Loan Fund asking for all documents on programs for seven Latin-American countries. His staff had already obtained considerable information from sources outside ICA indicating mismanagement, conflicts of interest, and other corruption in the program in Peru.

A month later, on October 11, 1960, President Eisenhower issued a formal order denying access to the records Hardy had requested.

Three weeks later, on October 31, 1960, Chairman Hardy made a formal request for specific ICA documents from the Office of Inspector General and Comptroller. This set the groundwork for shutting off funds to the Office of Inspector General and Comptroller under the provisions of the 1960 Amendment to the Mutual Security Act cited earlier in this chapter.

President Eisenhower followed up a month later, on December 2, with a certification denying access to these OIGC documents and eighty other documents requested.

Here was the showdown to determine how far President Eisenhower would go in overriding the express provisions of the 1959 law establishing the Office of Inspector General and Comptroller. Chairman Hardy notified the GAO of the OIGC refusal to produce records. And Comptroller General Joseph Campbell, as head of GAO, filed notice that unless the documents were made available the funds for OIGC would be shut off on December 9.

By so doing, Campbell ruled that the refusal to produce the documents on foreign aid to Latin-American countries was a violation of the law even if the orders were issued by his one-time close associate, President Eisenhower.

On December 9, Gerald Morgan, Deputy Assistant to the President, requested a ruling from Attorney General William P. Rogers, and thirteen days later Rogers wrote President Eisenhower (see Appendix C). The Attorney General, as would be expected from his earlier espousal of the most extreme interpretation of "executive privilege," declared Comptroller General Campbell's ruling "erroneous." In his opinion, the President had a constitutional right to withhold whatever he wanted to withhold. Rogers advised President Eisenhower that he had the authority to direct the Secretary of the Treasury and the Secretary of State to disregard the ruling of the Comptroller General cutting off funds for the Office of Inspector General and Comptroller.

With this advice in hand, President Eisenhower, on December 23, overrode the disclosure provisions of the Mutual Security Act of 1959 and the ruling of the Comptroller General he had appointed. In letters to Secretary of Treasury Robert B. Anderson and to Secretary of State Christian Herter, President Eisenhower told them to use federal funds to pay the Office of Inspector General and Comptroller.

He called attention to Campbell's contention that such payments were to be cut off under the law passed in 1959, and added:

"This position, I am advised by the Attorney General, is based upon erroneous interpretation of law which would reach an unconstitutional result and that mutual security program funds continue to be made available for expenses of the Office of Inspector General and Comptroller.

"Accordingly, you are hereby directed, until the end of my term of office on January 20, 1961, to cause disbursements to be made for such expenses upon the receipt of certified vouchers presented for that purpose."

Chairman Hardy continued the investigation of Peru. But he had need for documents that would be crucial in establishing the degree of mismanagement and corruption in the ICA program there. The most he could do now was to hope for better success under the new administration. However, he did not want to present President-elect John F. Kennedy with a problem for solution on or before the January 20 inaugural ceremonies.

He talked to Theodore Sorenson, Administrative Assistant to Senator Kennedy and later counsel to the President, and informed him of the pending problem. Hardy stated that he would withdraw his request which could prevent payment of OIGC personnel if he received assurances from the President-elect that the new administration would review the problem immediately after the inaugural.

On December 31, 1960, Hardy received a telegram from President-elect Kennedy asking that he postpone action on the documents until the new administration had "an opportunity to review [the] situation." Hardy complied.

The night of January 18, 1961, President Eisenhower went before a nationwide audience to give his "farewell address." He appealed for an "alert and knowledgeable citizenry" to combat the military-industrial complex that could "endanger our liberties or democratic processes."

"This conjunction of an immense military establishment and a large arms industry is new in the American experience," President Eisenhower said. "The total influence—economic, political, even spiritual—is felt in every city, every statehouse, every office of the Government.

"We recognize the imperative need for this development. Yet we must not fail to comprehend its grave implications. Our toil, resources, and livelihood are all involved: so is the very structure of our society.

"In the council of Government, we must guard against the acquisition of unwarranted influence, whether sought or unsought, by the military-industrial complex. The potential for the disastrous rise of misplaced power exists and will persist."

[Congressman Edward Hebert, of Louisiana, had made a good many comments on the military-industrial complex, and he had conducted a fine investigation documenting some of the problems. But the record indicated Chairman Hebert had not received full co-operation from the Eisenhower administration. Now President Eisenhower was expressing as much concern as Hebert.]

"We must never let the weight of this combination endanger our liberties or democratic processes," President Eisenhower warned. "We should take nothing for granted. Only an alert and knowledgeable citizenry can compel the proper meshing of the huge industrial and military machinery of defense with our peaceful methods and goals, so that security and liberty may prosper together.

"Partly because of the huge costs involved, a Government contract becomes virtually a substitute for intellectual curiosity. For every old blackboard there are now hundreds of new electronic computers.

"The prospect of domination of the Nation's scholars by

Federal employment, project allocations, and the power of money is very present—and is gravely to be regarded."

President Eisenhower might have added that the arbitrary withholding of information from Congress and the public was the quickest way to give this military-industrial combination the control he believed to be so dangerous. He apparently had never understood the secrecy problem in his administration in such a way that he could see the connection between the increase in secrecy and the decrease in liberty and other essential elements of democracy. Chairman Hardy, I myself, and others hoped the new President would.

CHAPTER XVI

Kennedy Makes a Wobbly Start

President John F. Kennedy had been in office only ten days when he gave his "State of the Union" address on January 30, 1961. His comments on making information available to Congress were general in nature and seemingly consistent with his campaign pledges. President Kennedy said:

"Our Constitution wisely assigns both joint and separate roles to each branch of the Government; and a President and a Congress who hold each other in mutual respect will neither permit nor attempt any trespass. For my part, I shall withhold from neither the Congress nor the people any fact or report, past, present, or future, which is necessary for an informed judgment of our conduct or hazards. I shall neither shift the burden of executive decisions to the Congress, nor avoid responsibility for the outcome of those decisions."

President Kennedy was not so specific on the subject as Candidate Kennedy had been, nor was he as precise as the Democratic platform on "Freedom of Information." The Democratic platform said:

"We reject the Republican contention that the workings of government are the special private preserve of the Executive. The massive wall of secrecy erected between the Executive branch and the Congress as well as the citizen must be torn down. Information must flow freely, save in those areas in which the national security is involved."

During the 1960 campaign, President Kennedy made a

most forthright declaration on the responsibility of the President to keep the citizens fully informed so that democracy would flourish.

"An informed citizenry is the basis of representative government," he said. "Democracy—as we know it—cannot exist unless the American people are equipped with the information which is necessary if they are to make the informed political choices on which the proper functioning of the democracy depends. An informed people—able to examine, and when necessary, to criticize, its government—is the only guarantee of responsible democracy."

As a candidate, Kennedy also declared that the President had much more than a negative duty.

"The President—who himself bears much of the responsibility for the preservation of American democracy—has the affirmative duty to see that the American people are kept fully informed. It is true that in today's world of peril some Government information must be kept secret—information whose publication would endanger the security of national security—the people of the United States are entitled to the fullest possible information about their Government—and the President must see that they receive it."

Senator Kennedy said that the "executive privilege" should be reserved for the exclusive use of the President. He added that when information is not restricted by specific statute, security needs, or the Constitution, "there is no justification for using the doctrine of 'executive privilege' to withhold that information from Congress and the public."

On February 4—only two weeks after Kennedy's inauguration—Secretary of State Dean Rusk wrote Representative Porter Hardy.

"Just a note to let you know that we have not forgotten the question on the availability of records. I am working with our new legal adviser, Mr. Abram Chayes, and hope that he can be in touch with you during the coming week. Let me assure you that we will move on this matter as promptly as possible."

Chairman Hardy was now optimistic about gaining access to the reports and papers of the International Cooperation Administration programs in Peru and six other Latin-American nations. Three days later, Chayes called at Hardy's office, and the following day Chairman Hardy wrote a friendly little note to Secretary of State Rusk saying that he trusted the access problem "will be resolved quickly."

More than two weeks passed without action, however, and with each day Chairman Hardy became more irritated. On February 28, he wrote Rusk prodding him again on the need for the documents on foreign-aid programs in Brazil, Uruguay, Argentina, Chile, Bolivia, Peru, and Colombia. The subcommittee has "directed the staff to examine all executive branch documents and files relating to the U.S. aid operations in the aforesaid countries and to interview such department and agency personnel as may be necessary."

There was still no action from Secretary of State Rusk, and ten days later Hardy had reached the end of his patience. He wrote a letter to President Kennedy and delivered it to the White House to President Kennedy's appointment secretary, Kenneth O'Donnell.

It was a Friday afternoon, and O'Donnell informed Chairman Hardy he would put the letter in the President's hands the first thing Monday morning. Hardy said he felt this was important enough that it should be delivered to President Kennedy that day, for he planned to conduct hearings on the affair on Monday. O'Donnell said he would get the letter to the President immediately.

Hardy's letter informed President Kennedy of the background of delays, and the promise of the new administration made to find a speedy solution.

"Seven weeks have now elapsed since the inauguration and I have no reason to believe that a workable solution is any nearer than it was on December 9, 1960, under the former administration," Hardy wrote. "You may recall that it was on that date that the Comptroller General prohibited further use of program funds for expenses of the office of the Inspector General and Comptroller because of its failure to furnish my subcommittee with requested documents in accordance with . . . the Mutual Security Act of 1954, as amended."

Hardy was polite but direct:

"I regret the necessity of bringing this matter to your attention, and would be reluctant to intrude on your busy schedule if I were not aware of the importance of this matter to you. In this connection, I feel you should know that it is my present plan to hold a meeting of my subcommittee on Monday of next week to discuss the advisability of scheduling promptly a hearing to which Secretary Rusk would be invited to inform the subcommittee concerning the extent of cooperation which we can expect in securing the information necessary for us to discharge our constitutional and statutory responsibilities.

"As I am sure you are aware, I have made every effort to avoid the necessity of seeking a solution to the problem in this manner. However, I feel that the lack of success of other methods to date leaves me no alternative."

Before Hardy had reached his home, President Kennedy had called and left a number. This wasn't somebody calling for the President, but the President himself. Hardy returned the call, and was assured by President Kennedy that Secretary of State Rusk would be in touch with him. Rusk called a few minutes later, and promised immediate action on the information problem.

Hardy said that if he could be assured of getting some satisfactory discussions on Monday, he would be glad to wait until that day for official word from Rusk.

Rusk's letter of Monday, March 13, stated:

"The Department shares with you a deep concern that the foreign aid programs which are so important to the success of our foreign policy, should be administered effectively and in a manner that is above reproach.

"I have therefore directed the officers of the Department concerned to cooperate fully with you and your staff to expedite your investigation and to make available to you all information and documents relevant to your inquiry which we properly can."

Chairman Hardy took Secretary Rusk at his word and assumed that records would be made available. The next morning Hardy called Assistant Secretary Brooks Hays to inform him that a staff investigator would be visiting the office of the Inspector General and Comptroller with instructions to talk to personnel in that office. He asked that Hays do what he could to assure that Investigator Walton Woods receive a co-operative reception.

However, when Woods showed up at the office of Acting Inspector General James E. Nugent and asked to speak with Investigator Michael J. Ambrose he was refused permission. Nugent said that as far as he was concerned the orders under the Eisenhower administration were still in force, but that he would check with Legal Counsel Chayes to see if there had been a change. Later Woods returned to Nugent's office and was informed by Nugent that no files or documents from the Office of the Inspector General were to be made available to the subcommittee.

Chairman Hardy was amazed that the same roadblocks continued to exist. On March 16, 1961, he again wrote Rusk relating what had happened and commenting:

"In spite of these developments I cannot believe that this administration is disposed to adhere to the withholding policies of the prior administration."

Then Hardy let Rusk know that despite all the roadblocks put in the way of the subcommittee, information had already been obtained that raised serious questions about the operation of the ICA policing system.

"The data which we have already assembled independently give us reason to question whether either the Office of the Inspector General and Comptroller or its predecessor organization has performed in a satisfactory manner," Hardy wrote.

"An office like this, exercising as it does an internal watchdog function, is of particular concern to a subcommittee such as ours. For when the Congress can be assured that such an office is doing a good job, then the areas where independent congressional inquiry may be required become fewer and smaller, and the work of Congress is accordingly simplified. Certainly we cannot evaluate the work of this office [OIGC] in any particular, if we are not permitted full access to its files and interviews with its personnel."

When Chairman Hardy called a hearing five days later on March 21, the witnesses showed up with letters of instructions flatly barring testimony. Secretary of State Rusk supplied each witness with the form letter prohibiting free testimony "concerning the conduct of the foreign aid program in Peru.

"I am writing this letter to instruct you that you are not authorized to testify concerning the contents of any files of the International Cooperation Administration or the Office of the Inspector General and Comptroller in the Department of State which relates to an investigation into charges of misconduct on the part of individuals or corporate persons or, more generally, to testify concerning any matter involved in such an investigation carried on by the International Cooperation Administration or the Office of the Inspector General and Comptroller in the Department of State."

So this was what the Kennedy administration called "cooperation" to "expedite your investigation and to make available to you all information and documents relevant to your inquiry which we properly can." Chairman Hardy had hoped for better, but concluded that it was time to end the polite letter writing and get down to tough talk.

"Until this morning," he declared, "it was my sincere hope that we would see some real improvement."

Hardy had been frustrated for a full year in his effort to gain access to the key documents on foreign aid in Peru. And the Kennedy administration, in office already two months, had done nothing to change the system that covered up for the dishonest and the incompetent people who wasted foreign-aid funds. Worse yet, it developed that twelve witnesses Hardy called in carried identical letters of instructions from Rusk to refuse to testify or produce records on any investigations conducted by ICA.

Hardy denounced the Rusk letter as "the most arrogant instruction" ever given to government witnesses. Representative George Meader declared that "a curtain had been rung down" on the operations of the ICA.

Meader, the highest ranking Republican on the Hardy subcommittee, demanded that Secretary Rusk should be brought before the subcommittee to explain the barriers he was erecting against investigations by Congress.

When Chairman Hardy agreed to call Rusk the very next day, State Department officials said "it would be very difficult" for Rusk to appear at that time for he was leaving the following evening for Bangkok and a major international conference of the Southeast Asia Treaty Organization nations.

Hardy declared that Rusk would be summoned before the subcommittee when he returned from the international conference, and that in the meantime he would be calling all other responsible State Department officials in an effort to get to the bottom of the stalling.

For the record, he reviewed the long struggle to get information on the Peru program from the Eisenhower administration. He also related the details of the patient two-month wait to give the Kennedy administration sufficient time to examine the problem carefully.

Then, to light a fire under the issue, Chairman Hardy disclosed enough information to make it obvious that he was on the trail of multimillion-dollar scandals in the handling of foreign aid in Peru. He revealed that 2 million dollars in U.S. funds were spent on a farm-to-market highway which led only to unarable mountainous land. It was started before plans were completed, plans were changed while it was being constructed, and the funds ran out when it was only half finished.

He also told about an irrigation project built at Pampas de Noco. It cost $125,000 of Americans' money, but it didn't work because there simply was not enough water available in the area to make use of the projected irrigation works.

John R. Neale, director of the United States Operations Mission in Peru, had acquired a $200,000 interest in a ranching corporation that received aid under the U.S. program. Although Neale had resigned in 1958, there were indications that key ICA and State Department personnel had protected him from a thorough investigation for months.

Hardy revealed widespread irregularities in the 14-million-dollar drought relief program in Peru. He had testimony that as much as 60 per cent of the so-called "drought relief" went into unauthorized channels and was no help to the drought victims.

Chairman Hardy made certain that President Kennedy was apprised of the nature of the mismanagement and fraud being hidden by the State Department. The reaction was fast, and the Rusk letter of instructions was slapped down by the White House on direct orders from President Kennedy.

Brooks Hays, the former congressman and Assistant Secretary of State for Congressional Relations, assured Chairman

Hardy that the Rusk instructions would be rescinded, the documents released, and witnesses freed to testify.

Witnesses called by Hardy a week later, on March 29, did testify freely. These witnesses produced a letter from State Department Legal Counsel Abram J. Chayes instructing them to forget the whole thing. Chayes wrote:

"The instructions contained in the letter of March 21, 1961, addressed to you by Secretary of State Dean Rusk, are hereby withdrawn. In view of this fact, I would appreciate it if you would return the letter to me and treat it as though it had not been sent."

Nothing that Chayes could write, however, could erase from some people's minds the memory of this clumsy and arrogant effort of the State Department to withhold. To ensure its perpetuity, Representative Meader rose on the House floor two weeks later, on April 17, to recite the story for the *Congressional Record.*

"In recent years, ambitious bureaucrats have concocted and promoted the so-called doctrine of 'executive privilege,' which, in my judgment, is a myth," Meader said. "In my view, there is no right or power in the executive branch of the Government to decide what facts Congress needs concerning the conduct of the public business. . . . That decision is clearly and properly a legislative decision."

Meader declared that "the struggle between bureaucrats who wish to hide their activities and committees of Congress insisting on access to complete and accurate information concerning public business . . . has not received the attention it merits."

The Michigan congressman was a Republican, to be sure, but he was one of a handful who could not be accused of playing partisan politics with this issue. No man in Congress insisted any more aggressively than George Meader that the Eisenhower administration make records available to the public, to Congress and the General Accounting Office.

When Meader quoted President Kennedy's January 30 address on the state of the Union, he did not do so in a malicious or partisan manner.

Kennedy had said: "For my part, I shall withhold from neither the Congress nor the people, any fact or report, past, present or future, which is necessary for an informed judgment of our conduct and hazards."

"I wish this sentence could be printed in capital letters in the *Congressional Record*," Meader said. "Many of us welcomed that clear, forthright statement as heralding a new policy in the executive branch of the Government with respect to furnishing information to congressional committees on request."

Representative Meader was not critical of President Kennedy for the delays on Peru, for President Kennedy had personally overridden his Secretary of State. But Meader was wary of the future.

"As the bureaus and agencies in the executive branch of the Government have grown in number, and in power," he said, "there has been a parallel growth in their efforts to shroud in secrecy the manner in which they discharge their stewardship of the public authority and moneys entrusted to them."

Meader declared that "the question remained whether that laudable generality [in President Kennedy's address of January 30] would be actually carried out in practice" or whether there would be "procrastination and recalcitrance on the part of officials."

Within two weeks of the March 29, 1961, showdown, the Hardy subcommittee was receiving the documents on the U.S. aid program in Peru. These were the documents, the release of which Attorney General William P. Rogers had said "would gravely impair the proper functioning and administration of the executive branch of the Government."

What the reports did do was to document fully the sloppy,

wasteful, and corrupt administration of foreign aid in Peru.

From the outset the Peru drought relief program had been riddled with irregularities. There were shipments of 106,000 tons of grain meant to be sold to help needy drought victims but which were sold, without authorization, to pay administrative costs, port charges, and inland transportation costs. Above all, the grain was not meant to be sold, as it was, for the profiteering of grain millers in Peru. It wasn't to be sold to raise money to buy houses to be sold to influential Peruvians at less than cost.

The mismanagement of the program was so raw that it hadn't completely escaped detection in Washington. A desk officer in 1957 had figured that only 12,000 tons of the first 45,000 tons had been accounted for and asked: "Who received the rest of the grain?"

No one answered his question, however, either in the Washington ICA office or at the Embassy in Peru. When a Washington auditor was finally sent to Peru, he found that no end-use checks had been made by the United States Operations Mission (USOM). He stated:

"The lone USOM auditor, a local employee, stated that USOM officials issued orders that no checks were to be made beyond the offices of the committees selling [drought aid] foods. Thus, end users were not contacted and no determination could be made as to the proper utilization of food."

Within the State Department and the ICA no aggressive action was taken to find out whether there was any substance to the complaints of conflicts of interest, waste, and major misuse of funds. Lethargy, incompetence, excuses, and cover-up prevailed.

When Dr. Raymond C. Gibson, an employee of the Office of Education, returned from an official visit in Peru, he called attention of high officials of ICA to the activities of John R. Neale, head of the USOM in Peru, who had a large interest in a farm receiving benefits of ICA funds.

Instead of investigating Neale's holdings, top ICA officials characterized Gibson's complaint as "character assassination." The officials did assign an investigator to the case but told him to "assure Neale of our belief in his integrity."

Within a few months, the case had become known within ICA not as the Neale case, but the Gibson case. ICA started a full field background investigation of Dr. Gibson, and one official pledged to hold Dr. Gibson to "full accountability" for filing a complaint against Neale.

The ICA investigators overlooked information in the ICA files which disclosed that Neale's family had an interest in a Peru ranch. Continued complaints finally forced ICA hearings on Neale in 1958, but even then his character witnesses included the American Ambassador to Peru, Theodore Achilles, and Rollin S. Atwood, regional director of the Office of Latin-American Operations of the ICA.

"When Achilles and Atwood appeared before the ICA hearing board as character witnesses for Neale, they seemed more concerned with the motivations of the complainants than they were with the truth of their allegation," the report of the Hardy subcommittee stated.

"The high position of Neale and the high position of his uncritical supporters, Atwood and Achilles, somewhat cowed the investigators assigned to this case.

"At the time of his removal, Neale had been affiliated with the Bazo Corporation [the ranching operation] for over eight years, and for at least four of those years ICA had in its possession sufficient information to warrant an investigation which . . . would have turned up the basic facts.

"It was congressional intervention that precipitated the Guinane investigation"—the final investigation that brought about Neale's resignation.

"All employees of ICA seem to know, without being specifically instructed," the subcommittee report went on, "that the preferred policy of the agency, and the Embassy in this instance, is to brush this sort of instance under the rug, with a quiet 'resignation' or 'retirement.'"

"Although the old office of Personnel Security and Integrity in ICA was primarily responsible for the ineffective investigation in the Neale case, its successor, OIGC, did not perform with any more credit in a related matter."

The ICA had used "executive privilege" to cover up its failures for several years. Instead of learning from past failures, the agency continued its negligence with full confidence that "executive privilege" could hide the failures from Congress, the General Accounting Office and the public.

The details of the scandals had not been known to President Eisenhower, nor had he known of the incredible laxity in the investigative units in the ICA. However, by promoting a secrecy cloak for the investigators of ICA he had allowed the ICA to hide the major defects in a vital part of an agency administering approximately 4 billion dollars a year.

CHAPTER XVII

A Pending Problem for JFK

In its first year, the Kennedy administration had tackled the problem of secrecy with noble thoughts and brave deeds. President Kennedy could not have spoken more clearly on the need for open government in a democratic society. Moreover, he had followed up his words with stringent action by overruling Secretary of State Dean Rusk on the one occasion when the State Department had tried to hide records behind a claim of "executive privilege."

Chairman Edward Hebert said that his Armed Services subcommittee was receiving better co-operation than it had ever received from the Defense Department. Hebert had talked with President Kennedy and been assured that the administration felt it needed the help and prodding of a committee of Congress to cut the billions in wasteful defense spending.

The investigations by Chairman Porter Hardy were proceeding on the same note of co-operation, and the Virginia Democrat said he was "hopeful that it will continue." Chairman Hardy's subcommittee had a number of investigations of foreign aid under way, and he believed that some of these investigations would be a real test of the sincerity and consistency of the Kennedy administration stand on "executive privilege."

Though many good signs indicated the Kennedy administration meant what it said about an open information policy, there were other signs that did not augur so well. Perhaps the most important was President Kennedy's personal sensitivity to criticism and his inclination to try to punish those he regarded as being "enemies" or unfairly critical.

The President himself had telephoned reporters and editors to complain about stories he considered unfair or unfavorable to him or his administration. At one time, the reporters for *Time* magazine were cut off from contact with White House sources on a direct order from the President. The order was lifted in about two weeks, after President Kennedy and his assistants felt *Time's* reporters and editors had been given a lesson.

Other persons in the White House behaved even tougher, threatening retaliation against reporters they felt had done them damage. Lloyd Norman, Pentagon correspondent for *Newsweek* magazine, became the target of an FBI investigation when he beat his colleagues with an exclusive report on the alternative plans for action on the Berlin crisis. The investigation was instigated despite the fact that before publication the report was read by a high White House figure who raised no question as to the propriety of printing it.

A memorandum by Frederick G. Dutton, Special Assistant to the President, contained language on government information policies that "shocked" Representative John Moss. The Dutton memorandum of July 20, 1961, was attached to a Civil Service Commission statement on standards of conduct for government employees. It stated:

"Employees may not disclose official information without either appropriate general or specific authority under agency regulations."

Congressman Moss asked the White House for a "complete reversal" of the statement, plus a "positive directive to all employees to honor the people's right to know as a routine matter in the conduct of government business.

"This restrictive attitude expressed by this [Dutton] lan-

guage is a complete reversal of all of the policies which the
House government information subcommittee has supported
for many years," Moss wrote to Dutton. "It is also a direct
contradiction of the clear position which President Kennedy
has taken. . . ."

The White House immediately withdrew the Dutton
memorandum and asserted the right of the people to be informed about government operations. The incident nevertheless underscored the need for constant vigilance to prevent
directives that in substance tell government employees to
keep their mouths shut.

At the Pentagon there were also a few unhealthy signs that
bore watching. Defense Secretary Robert Strange McNamara was generally praised as a bright, able, and hard-work-
ing public official, but his performance in the information
area did not elicit equally laudatory comments. Though Mc-
Namara's press chief, Assistant Secretary of Defense Arthur
Sylvester, had served for years as a reporter in the Washington Bureau of the Newark *News*, he was sharply critical of
the press in his first months in office. He did little to smooth
the road for the Defense Secretary or to educate McNamara's
attitudes on freedom of information.

Testimony released in May 1961 by the Senate Committee
on Armed Services disclosed that McNamara appeared to
favor less information for the public as well as misinformation on our military developments.

"Why should we tell Russia that the Zeus development
may not be satisfactory?" McNamara asked the Armed Services Committee. "What we ought to be saying is that we
have the most perfect anti-ICBM system that the human
mind will ever devise. Instead, the public domain is already
full of statements that the Zeus may not be satisfactory, that
it has deficiencies. I think it is absurd to release that kind of
information."

The McNamara statement was met with immediate

criticism from Representative John E. Moss, chairman of the House Government Information Subcommittee. Moss, a Democrat, declared that McNamara's testimony was "a gross disservice" to the people of the United States and inconsistent with views expressed by President Kennedy. He asked how the McNamara statement could be reconciled with President Kennedy's pledge to "withhold from neither the Congress nor the people any fact or report, past, present or future, which is necessary for an informed judgment of our conduct and hazards."

Representative Moss declared that "advocacy of a program of misinformation constitutes a grave disservice to a nation already confused and suffering from informational malnutrition. To claim perfection in a weapon system, thereby creating a false sense of security, only results in complacency complained about by the very officials who would further feed it."

McNamara, Moss said, "expressed an attitude which while not new is nevertheless most alarming."

In the face of a barrage of similar criticism, the Defense Department hurriedly released a statement that McNamara did not mean to mislead the American people but only the Russians.

At his press conference on May 26, 1961, the Defense Secretary issued a four-point statement to serve as a guide on information policy. McNamara, forty-four-year-old Phi Beta Kappa and a former assistant professor of business administration at Harvard, had learned at least what his published position must be.

"In a democratic society," his clarification began, "the public must be kept informed of the major issues in our national defense policy."

While pointing out the need to avoid disclosure of information that might aid our potential enemies, he declared it "is equally important to avoid overclassification. I suggest that we follow this principle: When in doubt underclassify."

The Defense Secretary also said that public statements must reflect the policy of the Defense Department, and that Defense personnel should not discuss "foreign policy subjects, a field which is reserved for the President and the Secretary of State."

Representative Moss commended Defense Secretary McNamara for "recognition of the people's right to know." He singled out for praise the McNamara comment that "the public has at least as much right to bad news as good news." However, he reserved judgment on the instructions restricting comment on policy matters. Moss asked to be advised on all directives or other instructions used in implementing the general information policy. He had learned by now that fine policy statements can mask the most intolerable withholding of information.

The reasonableness of the general policy statements on Defense information could hardly be criticized, but complaints were beginning to be heard about a tightening of curbs on speeches by military officers and about the difficulty of access to personnel at the Pentagon.

The Navy Times, a private publication, commented:

"Americans generally ought to be having some misgivings over the current trend at the Pentagon. There's an air of secrecy, of censorship, of arbitrary rulings."

The Defense Department toyed with the idea of invoking "executive privilege" when two committees of Congress initiated investigations of shipments of strategic materials to various Iron Curtain countries. The Internal Security Subcommittee of the Senate and a House Select Committee on Export Control were embarking on a repetition of the East-West trade investigations that Robert Kennedy, then a committee lawyer, had directed five years earlier. As Attorney

General, Robert Kennedy advised against the use of "executive privilege."

Despite assurances that the Kennedy administration would not claim "executive privilege," Chairman Porter Hardy wanted the law to state that reports of the Inspector General and Comptroller on foreign-aid administration would be made available to Congress and the General Accounting Office (GAO) auditors. Promises were fine, but Chairman Hardy wanted a firm law to bolster his subcommittee's authority to obtain records on foreign-aid spending.

Hardy's amendment to the foreign-aid legislation of 1961 provided that if the Inspector General and Comptroller failed to make information available to Congress and the GAO auditors, their funds would be cut off by GAO. The House gave the amendment overwhelming support.

The Senate, however—with support from the Kennedy administration—emasculated the Hardy amendment by adding what Representative George Meader described as the "Presidential escape clause." This clause provided that the Executive can avoid furnishing information on foreign-aid expenditures upon a "certification by the President that he has forbidden the furnishing thereof pursuant to such request and his reason for so doing."

Representatives Hardy and Meader remembered the experience with a similar escape clause that was attached to the foreign-aid legislation of 1959. It had enabled President Eisenhower simply to sign a certification in order to bar Senate and House investigators from every key record they sought dealing with mismanagement of the foreign-aid program. The proof of the weakness of a law with such an escape clause had caused the Congress to pass the tight Hardy amendment in 1960. Although President Eisenhower defied the specific intent of the Hardy amendment by hiding the Peru foreign-aid records, the 1960 provisions had been considered strong enough for a court test if Eisenhower had remained in office.

The Kennedy administration's support of the "Presidential escape clause" in the 1961 legislation was a bad omen to Representative Meader.

"The effect of the Presidential escape clause . . ." he said, "is to weaken existing law and to diminish the power the Congress enjoyed during [the last year of] the Eisenhower administration to obtain information from the Executive of foreign aid expenditures.

"This constitutes a victory for the bureaucrats, a defeat for Congress, and a serious setback in the fight against government secrecy."

Criticism of the Kennedy administration from some Republicans could be disregarded. But from George Meader it invited serious attention. As the foregoing chapters have shown, he was one of the most outspoken critics of the information policies of the Eisenhower administration.

Meader had joined Representative Hardy, a Democrat, in criticizing the State Department in March when Secretary of State Rusk issued orders barring the Hardy committee from testimony or records on the Peru scandals. But he had also joined Hardy in applauding President Kennedy for overruling his own Secretary of State and making the ICA records on Peru foreign-aid scandals available to the Hardy subcommittee.

On July 28, 1961, the Democratic-controlled House Government Operations Committee issued a report on information policies. It was, of course, highly critical of the Eisenhower administration but not completely approving of the new administration. The committee found the record of the first months of the Kennedy administration "mixed." However, it saw a "hopeful note" in the fact that President Kennedy had given "positive policy direction from the top." The report contained a favorable comment on "the Presidential determination—even at the cost of reversing his Secretary of State—to live up to the new administration's pledge to honor the right to know."

Democrats took great party pride in the speeches President Kennedy made to assure the public of his concern for freedom of information.

"The essence of free communication must be that our failures as well as our successes will be broadcast around the world," President Kennedy said at the convention of the National Association of Broadcasters. "And therefore we take double pride in our successes.

"The great inner resource of freedom, the resource which has kept the world's oldest democracy continuously young and vital, the resource which has always brought us our greatest exploits in time of our greatest need, is the very fact of the open society.

"Thus, if we are once again to preserve our civilization, it will be because of our freedom, and not in spite of it. . . . For the flow of ideas, the capacity to make informed choices, the ability to criticize, all the assumptions upon which political democracy rests, depends largely upon communication."

By the time the House Government Operations Committee was ready to file a second report on government information policies, the Democrats were aglow with admiration for President Kennedy. The September 21, 1961, report stated: "For the first time since the subcommittee entered the fight against excessive Government secrecy six years ago, there is a powerful new weapon—the support of a President who is clearly on record in favor of the greatest flow of Government information."

Representative Meader thought the Democrats were too willing to praise a Democratic administration. In his dissent, he wrote:

"I cannot subscribe to the majority report because in my judgment it has political overtones and accepts the self-serving declarations of officials in the new administration rather than actual performance as indicating an improvement in the attitude of the executive branch toward providing information to the Congress and the public.

"The majority condemns the Eisenhower administration record on secrecy in government while praising that of the Kennedy administration. Such a distinction in my opinion, is not justified."

Meader well remembered the fine words spoken in 1952 and 1953 on the same subject by officials of the Eisenhower administration. He knew that the true test of the Kennedy administration lay not with words but with the administration's continued willingness to support the power of inquiry of the Congress.

A few days after the release of the House report and Meader's dissent, Attorney General Kennedy upheld the importance of investigations by Congress.

On the "Meet the Press" television show on September 24, James Reston, Bureau Chief for The New York *Times*, said to Attorney General Kennedy:

"In the field of 'executive privilege' . . . you seem more willing than previous Presidents and administrations to give information sought by Congress."

"As far as 'executive privilege' is concerned," the Attorney General answered, "I was associated with a congressional committee for five or six years and had battles with the executive branch of the government regarding obtaining information.

"I think it is terribly important to insure that the executive branch of the government is not corrupt and that they are efficient, that the legislative branch of the government has the ability to check on what we are doing in the executive branch of the government.

"So, in every instance that has been brought to our attention in the Department of Justice so far by various departments of the executive branch where this question has been raised we have suggested and recommended that they make the information available to Congress. We will continue to do that. I don't say that there might not be an instance where 'executive privilege' might be used, but I think it is terribly important that the executive branch of the government, as powerful and strong as it is, that there be some check and balance on it, and in the last analysis the group that can best check and insure that it is handling its affairs properly is the Congress of the United States, so we will lean over backwards to make sure that they get the information they request."

There was no reason to doubt the sincerity of the youthful Attorney General, and in fact there was every reason to believe he meant what he said. He was speaking from personal experience, he seemed to speak with conviction, and it was not yet time to be posturing for the 1964 political campaign.

It was, of course, relatively easy to take a broad view at this time when opening records could only expose crimes or mismanagement that had developed when the Eisenhower administration was in power. It would take more courage and great understanding of government to open records that might expose a trusted Kennedy subordinate or embarrass the Kennedy administration.

Barely more than a year after the Kennedy administration had taken office, a situation arose which raised grave question as to what its long-range policy would be. In February 1962, during the hearings on alleged muzzling of military officers, President Kennedy invoked the claim of "executive privilege" at the request of Defense Secretary Robert McNamara. McNamara wished to avoid identifying for the Senate Preparedness Subcommittee the Pentagon officials who had censored specific speeches by high military officers.

President Kennedy's letter to McNamara of February 8, 1962 (see Appendix D), set out an ill-defined claim that the national interest was at stake. The letter contained some terminology that seemed to claim an absolute right to bar testimony before Congress by any subordinate career officials. It was attacked by Senator Strom Thurmond, the South Carolina Democrat, as a "dangerous" precedent that would have barred Congress from investigating the Pearl Harbor disaster or obtaining information on a wide variety of scandals.

Many political writers excused President Kennedy. Some pointed to language in the letter they said indicated that he was not setting a broad precedent but was merely shutting off an investigation they considered to be senseless. Representative Moss declared that the Senate subcommittee had the legal right to ask the questions to determine which censors had blue-penciled which speeches.

It was not clear immediately whether the February 8 letter was to be an isolated incident or a troublesome broad precedent for more arbitrary secrecy in the tradition of the May 17, 1954, Eisenhower letter.

CHAPTER XVIII

A Solution

History establishes that any administration may be afflicted with laxity, incompetence, and even outright fraud. History has also taught that any administration can harbor men who want to hide mistakes and corruption.

It is true that no President has been directly involved in fraudulent activity, and it seems unlikely that any ever will be. Holding such a high office would inspire almost any man to rise above the desire for personal enrichment, particularly if the cost might be damaging to his place in history. But any President might be tempted to hide records on a claim of "executive privilege" if he felt he could save some trusted subordinate from the slings of the opposition political party.

In varying degrees, our Presidents have been dependent upon a palace guard. The nature of the position, with all its vast responsibilities, makes a circle of close advisers inevitable. Thus Presidents of the past have sought information about alleged improprieties or corruptions from the very men who have been accused of perpetrating them. Instead of facts and a clear analysis of the problem—whether it was Teapot Dome, tax scandals, or Dixon-Yates—the Presidents have received misinformation and excuses. The accusations have been explained away to our Presidents as partisan complaints from politicians maliciously bent on destroying the administration's programs. Such explanations from palace guards unfortunately have been all too effective and have obscured the facts that would have alerted our Presidents to conflicts of interest, favoritism, and fraud.

President Kennedy and future Presidents will face the same kind of pitfalls. Regardless of their own integrity, they cannot be expected to conduct personal investigations of each of their subordinates. The Presidents and the people must therefore depend upon investigations from outside the executive branch—by the Congress and the General Accounting Office—for an aggressive search for the facts.

Investigations by Congress have demonstrated the failure of the military departments to police themselves effectively from the inside. In every recent year, the Congress and the GAO have pinpointed the waste of hundreds of millions of dollars on inefficient, incompetent, or corrupt handling of Defense contract arrangements.

Examination of testimony on the foreign-aid programs in Laos and Peru shows that the State Department is little better than the Defense Department in rooting out mismanagement and corruption. There are dozens of other areas within the bureaucracy where the record is just as bad.

It is doubtful that we will ever eliminate corruption in the federal government, but it must be kept under closer control or it can spread with devastating impact. Nothing speeds the growth of corruption more than policies that foster arbitrary secrecy. Secrecy allows little scandals to become major scandals, costly to the taxpayers, devastating to our foreign-aid program, to our position of defense readiness, and to our national morale.

"Secrecy," as the House Government Operations Committee has put it, "is the handmaiden of bureaucracy, especially military bureaucracy. It has so pervasive an effect that all government becomes invested with the urge to restrict—even those routine agencies which should be wide open to the public."

In these pages, I have not attempted to examine every

agency of government. I have examined enough, however, to show how severe the infection of secrecy has become, what dire symptoms it produces, and how seriously it threatens the health of our democracy.

It can be wiped out. As treatment for a permanent cure, I suggest the following steps:

1 *All officials except the President should be obligated to explain all their actions to Congress and the General Accounting Office, unless specific laws are passed for withholding information.* This does not mean that the public or Congress should have access to all papers when a decision is pending, but at a later date Congress should have access to all records and testimony concerning events leading up to the executive decisions.

A good example from recent history that shows the value of a properly conducted hearing was the Senate investigation of President Truman's firing of General Douglas MacArthur in 1951.

The special Senate committee—selected with a reasonably even division of political forces from the Armed Services and Foreign Relations committees—did not seek testimony from President Truman. However, it did require the testimony of General Omar Bradley, the Chairman of the Joint Chiefs of Staff. Bradley testified on all events leading up to the firing, including his meeting with President Truman. Bradley was not asked to recount verbatim his discussion with President Truman, but he testified he met with President Truman, that the MacArthur actions were discussed, and the decision was made by President Truman to fire General MacArthur.

The special Senate committee met behind closed doors but released a daily transcript of testimony that had been examined to eliminate any matter that might violate national military security standards.

Had the Eisenhower administration's doctrine of "executive privilege" prevailed at that time, a total secrecy blanket could have been thrown around the Defense Department, the Joint Chiefs of Staff, and the White House. There would have been no way of determining the facts leading up to the decision, except as the President found it convenient to reveal them.

How much better it was for all concerned that the MacArthur firing was carefully examined and that the public was apprised of all the material facts.

2 *Congress should enact special laws to cover the specific areas in which withholding of records is deemed necessary to the public good.* There are now laws that provide for withholding of federal income tax information from the public, and from all committees of Congress except certain ones with supervisory jurisdiction over the Internal Revenue Service. Laws have been enacted providing for withholding of Defense information that involves national security. Other areas—FBI reports, patent secrets, business reports, or personnel files—could be covered by special legislation of a similar nature, but modified to meet the requirements of the area in which the withholding is needed.

3 *Congress should provide stiff criminal penalties for use against government officials who withhold information from properly authorized committees of Congress or the GAO.* This legislation should also provide the mechanism for prosecution to be initiated by the Congress or the GAO. Such a mechanism is necessary to avoid the situation wherein an Attorney General, advocate for the President and appointed by the President, simply refuses to enforce the law or gives patently false legal opinions to avoid enforcement.

4 *The Congress should establish an effective means for systematic review of papers carrying national security classifications of "confidential," "secret," or "top secret." Or the President could establish a small committee to spot-check, review, and challenge questionable use of national security classifications.* However the review group is set up, its mem-

bers should be selected from outside the military field, and they should be persons with a strong and responsible interest in open government. They should have authority to challenge arbitrary or questionable security classifications and authority to obtain explanations from all persons with a role in questionable classifications.

This review group should not have the power to change classifications, only the power to recommend changes. It should have the authority, however, to file reports with Congress, with department heads, and with the President that could be made public. Such reports should identify individuals engaged in arbitrary or questionable overclassification, as well as those responsible for failing to take steps to declassify.

Only through the establishment of these checks on executive secrecy can the public be assured that laws are administered in the way that the Congress intended them to be. Only in this way can the public be certain that the laws are not twisted or disregarded by an arbitrary bureaucracy operating in secret.

And what about checks upon possible abuses by the investigating committees of Congress? There are many. The courts offer some of the most effective. Rulings in recent years have put limitations on the power of an investigating committee. The committee must be properly authorized by the House or Senate, with a specific authority, and it must operate within the scope of that authority. The courts will not uphold a contempt citation if a committee of Congress is operating outside its proper authority, or if the questions asked are not pertinent to the inquiry. Recent rulings have held that the committee chairman must also explain to the witness the reasons why the questions are pertinent and necessary to carry out the legislative function.

In addition to these legal limitations, committees of Congress are held in check by their own bipartisanship and the fact that they usually operate in the public view. The members of the committees nearly always represent a cross section of the Congress, everything from extreme liberals to extreme conservatives with many gradations between. This representation assures a spokesman for almost every point of view. It also assures cross examination of witnesses in most cases, for minority counsel is normally provided to help minority members bring out facts that the majority may choose to overlook or minimize.

In recent years, most committees have adopted rules of procedure to assure some element of fair play. Since most hearings are held in public, there is the opportunity for the press and other interested groups and individuals to view the questioning and to point out any lapses in fair play.

Open congressional hearings do not absolutely assure fair play, but they do represent the best practical means this country has so far devised for assuring the public's right to know about the running of its government.

It is pertinent to note here that in England, which is generally regarded by political authorities as a model for democratic procedures, the need for constant inquiry into governmental policies and administration of the laws is fully recognized.

The British Government, unlike ours, is totally responsible to the Parliament, with the Prime Minister and other ministers coming out of the Parliament. This system has resulted in the development of a number of devices to accomplish the same basic purpose that our congressional investigations should accomplish.

There is a "question time" in Parliament four days a week during which any member of the House of Commons may interrogate the various ministers and even the Prime Minister. This periodic opportunity for questioning makes it possible for the opposition either to obtain immediate answers or to demonstrate evasiveness on crucial issues.

Also the Parliament is free to investigate through select committees of the House of Commons which are unlimited in their power to compel testimony and production of records and to punish for contempt. The contempt can be punished by jailing by the Parliament for the duration of the term, and British courts have left this power unlimited over the years.

The "question time" and select committees are supplemented by Royal Commissions of Inquiry, technically established and appointed by the Crown and Tribunals of Inquiry, established by the Parliament with members named by the Crown.

The Royal Commissions have had no power to compel testimony and production of records. However, co-operation is usually obtained because of the pressure of British public opinion, as well as the ever-present threat that a select committee of the Commons can take jurisdiction and use its contempt powers to force testimony.

The Tribunals of Inquiry operate with the normal court powers of subpoena and oaths to compel testimony. This is a device for taking an inquiry out of the partisan political atmosphere of a legislative investigation.

In the United States the question is often asked whether greater congressional freedom in questioning officials of the executive branch would not interfere with the efficiency of the government. Much of the business of federal government is simply keeping records and preparing testimony to account for the custodianship of the government agencies. In most instances it would take an official far less time to go before a committee of Congress and give a frank account of the activities of his agency than it has taken to devise cover-ups for frauds, mismanagement, and embarrassing oversights.

The Teapot Dome scandals could have been fully disclosed

in a few months instead of several years. The details of some of the Truman tax scandals could have been uncovered in a few weeks. And again, a frank accounting could have explained the Dixon-Yates contract in a matter of days.

Congress can be of great service to a cabinet officer in keeping his agency clean. If a congressional committee is unreasonable, or brutal, or oversteps its jurisdiction, such abuses, it must be remembered, take place in public where they can be seen and remedied. The President and others in the executive branch have the personnel and facilities for pointing out the abuses so they can be eradicated in the face of public opinion.

Ours was designed to be a government of laws, and not a government of men. It was not intended that the President or any other official would have a right to disregard the laws of Congress in accounting on government activity. The President, it should be pointed out, has all of the protection he needs to prevent Congress from unduly interfering with him in carrying out his executive responsibilities. The separation of powers of the three branches of government is clearly set out in the Constitution, and the only way the Constitution has provided for Congress to take action against the President is to impeach him. Since no President yet has been impeached, this procedure would be resorted to in only the most drastic of circumstances.

The President of the United States, with the vast power and prestige of his office, has the obligation to set a tone of government that assures the fullest possible flow of information consistent with the nation's security. He must take the lead in breaking down the arrogance of the bureaucracy that assumes a right to keep the knowledge of the people's business from the people themselves, and thus restore the people's faith in their governmental servants.

President Kennedy has made an uncertain start. Whether he succeeds depends not only on him, but on the press and the public as well. We cannot afford to allow our faith in a President's good intentions and his own personal integrity to blind us, as we did during President Eisenhower's administration, to the machinations of the Washington cover-up. The press, the Congress, the public must make certain that Attorney General Kennedy and other key members of the Kennedy administration remember how "terribly important" it is that Congress and the Government Accounting Office maintain full access to the records of government.

When the old secrecy practices are cast aside and the freedom of information guaranteed, then will our democracy flourish as the founding fathers intended it should.

APPENDIX A

Letter from President Eisenhower
to the Secretary of Defense

THE WHITE HOUSE,
May 17, 1954

The Honorable the SECRETARY OF DEFENSE,
Washington, D. C.

DEAR MR. SECRETARY: It has long been recognized that to assist the Congress in achieving its legislative purposes every Executive Department or Agency must, upon the request of a Congressional Committee, expeditiously furnish information relating to any matter within the jurisdiction of the Committee, with certain historical exceptions—some of which are pointed out in the attached memorandum from the Attorney General. This Administration has been and will continue to be diligent in following this principle. However, it is essential to the successful working of our system that the persons entrusted with power in any one of the three great branches of Government shall not encroach upon the authority confided to the others. The ultimate responsibility for the conduct of the Executive branch rests with the President.

Within this Constitutional framework each branch should cooperate fully with each other for the common good. However, throughout our history the President has withheld information whenever he found that what was sought was confidential or its disclosure would be incompatible with the public interest or jeopardize the safety of the Nation.

Because it is essential to efficient and effective administration that employees of the Executive Branch be in a position to be completely candid in advising with each other on official matters, and because it is not in the public interest that any of their conversations or communications, or any documents or reproductions, concerning such advice be disclosed, you will instruct employees of your Department that in all of their appearances before the Subcommittee of the Senate Committee on Government Operations regarding the inquiry now before it they are not to testify to any such conversations or communications or to produce any such documents or reproductions. This principle must be maintained regardless of who would be benefited by such disclosures.

I direct this action so as to maintain the proper separation of powers

itional law is that all the powers entrusted to the government are
and the Judicial. It is essential to the successful working of this system
that the persons entrusted with power in any one of these branches
shall not be permitted to encroach upon the powers confided to the
others, but that each shall be limited to the exercise of the powers
appropriate to its own department and no other. The doctrine of
separation of powers was adopted to preclude the exercise of arbi-

This fundamental principle was fully recognized by our first President, George Washington, as early as 1796 when he said: ". . . it is
essential to the due administration of the Government that the bound-
should be preserved. . . ." In his Farewell Address, President Wash-
by one department into the domain of another as leading to despotism.
This principle has received steadfast adherence throughout the many
years of our history and growth. More than ever, it is our duty today
to heed these words if our country is to retain its place as a leader

For over 150 years—almost from the time that the American form
Presidents have established, by precedent, that they and members of
their Cabinet and other heads of executive departments have an un-
tory abounds in countless illustrations of the refusal, on occasion, by
the President and heads of departments to furnish papers to Congress,
or its committees, for reasons of public policy. The messages of our

past Presidents reveal that almost every one of them found it necessary to inform Congress of his constitutional duty to execute the office of President, and, in furtherance of that duty, to withhold information and papers for the public good.

Nor are the instances lacking where the aid of a court was sought in vain to obtain information or papers from a President and the heads of departments. Courts have uniformly held that the President and the heads of departments have an uncontrolled discretion to withhold the information and papers in the public interest, they will not interfere with the exercise of that discretion, and that Congress has not the power, as one of the three great branches of the Government, to subject the Executive Branch to its will any more than the Executive Branch may impose its unrestrained will upon the Congress.

PRESIDENT WASHINGTON'S ADMINISTRATION

In March 1792, the House of Representatives passed the following resolution:

"*Resolved,* That a committee be appointed to inquire into the causes of the failure of the late expedition under Major General St. Clair, and that the said committee be empowered to call for such persons, papers, and records, as may be necessary to assist their inquiries" (3 Annals of Congress, p. 493).

This was the first time that a committee of Congress was appointed to look into a matter which involved the Executive Branch of the Government. The expedition of General St. Clair was under the direction of the Secretary of War. The expenditures connected therewith came under the Secretary of the Treasury. The House based its right to investigate on its control of the expenditures of public moneys. It appears that the Secretaries of War and the Treasury appeared before the committee. However, when the committee was bold enough to ask the President for the papers pertaining to the General St. Clair campaign, President Washington called a meeting of his Cabinet (Binkley, *President and Congress,* pp. 40–41).

Thomas Jefferson, as Secretary of State, reports what took place at that meeting. Besides Jefferson, Alexander Hamilton, Henry Knox, Secretary of War, and Edmond Randolph, the Attorney General, were present. The Committee had first written to Knox for the original letters, instructions, etc., to General St. Clair. President Washington stated that he had called his Cabinet members together, because it was the first example of a demand on the Executive for papers, and he wished that so far as it should become a precedent, it should be rightly conducted. The President readily admitted that he did not doubt the propriety of what the House was doing, but he could conceive that there might be papers of so secret a nature that they ought

not to be given up. Washington and his Cabinet came to the unanimous conclusion:

"First, that the House was an inquest, and therefore might institute
inquiries. Second, that it might call for papers generally. Third, that
the Executive ought to communicate such papers as the public good
would permit, and ought to refuse those, the disclosure of which
would injure the public; consequently were to exercise a discretion.
Fourth, that neither the committee nor House had a right to call on
the Head of a Department, who and whose papers were under the
President alone; but that the committee should instruct their chairman
to move the House to address the President."

The precedent thus set by our first President and his Cabinet was
followed in 1796, when President Washington was presented with a
resolution of the House of Representatives which requested him to lay
before the House a copy of the instructions to the Minister of the
United States who negotiated the treaty with the King of Great Britain,
together with the correspondence and documents relative to that
treaty. Apparently it was necessary to implement the treaty with an
appropriation which the House was called upon to vote. The House
insisted on its right to the papers requested, as a condition to appropriating the required funds (*President and Congress,* Wilfred E. Binkley [1947], p. 44).

President Washington's classic reply was, in part, as follows:

"I trust that no part of my conduct has ever indicated a disposition
to withhold any information which the Constitution has enjoined upon
the President as a duty to give, or which could be required of him by
either House of Congress as a right; and with truth I affirm that it has
been, as it will continue to be while I have the honor to preside in the
Government, my constant endeavor to harmonize with the other
branches thereof so far as the trust delegated to me by the people of
the United States and my sense of the obligation it imposes to 'preserve,
protect, and defend the Constitution' will permit" (Richardson, *Messages and Papers of the Presidents,* vol. 1, p. 194).

Washington then went on to discuss the secrecy required in negotiations with foreign governments, and cited that as a reason for vesting
the power of making treaties in the President, with the advice and
consent of the Senate. He felt that to admit the House of Representatives into the treatymaking power, by reason of its constitutional duty
to appropriate monies to carry out a treaty, would be to establish a
dangerous precedent. He closed his message to the House as follows:

"As, therefore, it is perfectly clear to my understanding that the
assent of the House of Representatives is not necessary to the validity of
a treaty; . . . and as it is essential to the due administration of the
Government that the boundaries fixed by the Constitution between the
different departments should be preserved, a just regard to the Con-

stitution and to the duty of my office, under all the circumstances of this case, forbids a compliance with your request" (Richardson, *Messages and Papers of the Presidents,* vol. 1, p. 196).

PRESIDENT JEFFERSON'S ADMINISTRATION

In January 1807, Representative Randolph introduced a resolution, as follows:

"*Resolved,* That the President of the United States be, and he hereby is, requested to lay before this House any information in possession of the Executive, except such as he may deem the public welfare to require not to be disclosed, touching any illegal combination of private individuals against the peace and safety of the Union, or any military expedition planned by such individuals against the territories of any Power in amity with the United States; together with the measures which the Executive has pursued and proposes to take for suppressing or defeating the same" (16 Annals of Congress [1806–1807], p. 336).

The resolution was overwhelmingly passed. The Burr conspiracy was then stirring the country. Jefferson had made it the object of a special message to Congress wherein he referred to a military expedition headed by Burr. Jefferson's reply to the resolution was a Message to the Senate and House of Representatives. Jefferson brought the Congress up to date on the news which he had been receiving concerning the illegal combination of private individuals against the peace and safety of the Union. He pointed out that he had recently received a mass of data, most of which had been obtained without the sanction of an oath so as to constitute formal and legal evidence. "It is chiefly in the form of letters, often containing such a mixture of rumors, conjectures, and suspicions as renders it difficult to sift out the real facts and unadvisable to hazard more than general outlines, strengthened by concurrent information or the particular credibility of the relator. In this state of the evidence, delivered sometimes, too, under the restriction of private confidence, neither safety nor justice will permit the exposing names, except that of the principal actor, whose guilt is placed beyond question" (Richardson, *Messages and Papers of the Presidents,* vol. 1, p. 412, dated January 22, 1807).

SIMILAR ACTIONS BY PRESIDENTS JACKSON, TYLER, BUCHANAN, AND GRANT

On February 10, 1835, President Jackson sent a message to the Senate wherein he declined to comply with the Senate's resolution requesting him to communicate copies of charges which had been made to the President against the official conduct of Gideon Fitz, late

Surveyor-General, which caused his removal from office. The resolution stated that the information requested was necessary both in the action which it proposed to take on the nomination of a successor to Fitz, and in connection with the investigation which was then in progress by the Senate respecting the frauds in the sales of public lands.

The President declined to furnish the information. He stated that in his judgment the information related to subjects exclusively belonging to the executive department. The request therefore encroached on the constitutional powers of the executive.

The President's message referred to many previous similar requests, which he deemed unconstitutional demands by the Senate:

"Their continued repetition imposes on me, as the representative and trustee of the American people, the painful but imperious duty of resisting to the utmost any further encroachment on the rights of the Executive" (ibid., p. 133).

The President next took up the fact that the Senate resolution had been passed in executive session, from which he was bound to presume that if the information requested by the resolution were communicated, it would be applied in secret session to the investigation of frauds in the sales of public lands. The President said that, if he were to furnish the information, the citizen whose conduct the Senate sought to impeach would lose one of his basic rights, namely—that of a public investigation in the presence of his accusers and of the witnesses against him. In addition, compliance with the resolution would subject the motives of the President, in the case of Mr. Fitz, to the review of the Senate when not sitting as judges on an impeachment; and even if such a consequence did not follow in the present case, the President feared that compliance by the Executive might thereafter be quoted as a precedent for similar and repeated applications.

"Such a result, if acquiesced in, would ultimately subject the independent constitutional action of the Executive in a matter of great national concernment to the domination and control of the Senate; . . .

"I therefore decline a compliance with so much of the resolution of the Senate as requests 'copies of the charges, if any,' in relation to Mr. Fitz, and in doing so must be distinctly understood as neither affirming nor denying that any such charges were made . . ." (ibid., p. 134).

One of the best reasoned precedents of a President's refusal to permit the head of a department to disclose confidential information to the House of Representatives is President Tyler's refusal to communicate to the House of Representatives the reports relative to the affairs of the Cherokee Indians and to the frauds which were alleged to have been practiced upon them. A resolution of the House of Representatives had called upon the Secretary of War to communicate to the House the reports made to the Department of War by Lieutenant Colonel Hitchcock relative to the affairs of the Cherokee Indians together with all information communicated by him concerning the frauds he was charged to investigate; also all facts in the possession of the Executive relating to the subject. The Secretary of War consulted with the President and under the latter's direction informed the House that negotiations were then pending with the Indians for settlement of their claims; in the opinion of the President and the Department, therefore, publication of the report at that time would be inconsistent with the public interest. The Secretary of War further stated in his answer to the resolution that the report sought by the House, dealing with alleged frauds which Lieutenant Colonel Hitchcock was charged to investigate, contained information which was obtained by Colonel Hitchcock by ex parte inquiries of persons whose statements were without the sanction of an oath, and which the persons implicated had had no opportunity to contradict or explain. The Secretary of War expressed the opinion that to promulgate those statements at that time would be grossly unjust to those persons, and would defeat the object of the inquiry. He also remarked that the Department had not been given at that time sufficient opportunity to pursue the investigation, to call the parties affected for explanations, or to determine on the measures proper to be taken.

The answer of the Secretary of War was not satisfactory to the Committee on Indian Affairs of the House, which claimed the right to demand from the Executive and heads of departments such information as may be in their possession relating to subjects of the deliberations of the House.

President Tyler in a message dated January 31, 1843, vigorously asserted that the House of Representatives could not exercise a right to call upon the Executive for information, even though it related to a subject of the deliberations of the House, if, by so doing, it attempted to interfere with the discretion of the Executive.

The same course of action was taken by President James Buchanan in 1860 in resisting a resolution of the House to investigate whether the President or any other officer of the Government had, by money, patronage, or other improper means sought to influence the action of Congress for or against the passage of any law relating to the rights of any state or territory. (See Richardson, *Messages and Papers of the Presidents*, vol. 5, pp. 618–19.)

In the administration of President Ulysses S. Grant the House requested the President to inform it whether any executive offices, acts, or duties, and if any, what, have been performed at a distance from the seat of government established by law. It appears that the purpose of this inquiry was to embarrass the President by reason of his having spent some of the hot months at Long Branch. President Grant replied that he failed to find in the Constitution the authority given to the House of Representatives, and that the inquiry had nothing to do with legislation (Richardson, *Messages and Papers of the Presidents,* vol. 7, pp. 362–63).

PRESIDENT CLEVELAND'S ADMINISTRATION

In 1886, during President Cleveland's administration, there was an extended discussion in the Senate with reference to its relations to the Executive caused by the refusal of the Attorney General to transmit to the Senate certain documents concerning the administration of the Office of the District Attorney for the Southern District of South Alabama, and suspension of George W. Durkin, the late incumbent. The majority of the Senate Committee on the Judiciary concluded that it was entitled to know all that officially exists or takes place in any of the departments of Government and that neither the President nor the head of a department could withhold official facts and information as distinguished from private and unofficial papers.

In his reply President Cleveland disclaimed any intention to withhold official papers, but he denied that papers and documents inherently private or confidential, addressed to the President or a head of a department, having reference to an act entirely executive such as the suspension of an official, were changed in their nature and became official when placed for convenience in the custody of a public department. (Richardson, *Messages and Papers of the Presidents,* vol. 8, pp. 378–79, 381.)

Challenging the attitude that because the executive departments were created by Congress the latter had any supervisory power over them, President Cleveland declared (Eberling, *Congressional Investigation,* p. 258):

"I do not suppose that the public offices of the United States are regulated or controlled in their relations to either House of Congress by the fact that they were created by laws enacted by themselves. It must be that these instrumentalities were created for the benefit of the people and to answer the general purposes of government under the Constitution and the laws, and that they are unencumbered by any lien in favor of either branch of Congress growing out of their construction, and unembarrassed by any obligation to the Senate as the price of their creation."

PRESIDENT THEODORE ROOSEVELT'S ADMINISTRATION

In 1909, during the administration of President Theodore Roosevelt, the question of the right of the President to exercise complete direction and control over heads of executive departments was raised again.

At that time the Senate passed a resolution directing the Attorney General to inform the Senate whether certain legal proceedings had been instituted against the United States Steel Corporation, and if not, the reasons for its nonaction. Request was also made for any opinion of the Attorney General, if one was written. President Theodore Roosevelt replied refusing to honor this request upon the ground that "Heads of the Executive Departments are subject to the Constitution, and to the laws passed by the Congress in pursuance of the Constitution, and to the directions of the President of the United States, but to no other direction whatever" (*Congressional Record,* vol. 43, pt. 1, 60th Cong., 2d sess., pp. 527–28).

When the Senate was unable to get the documents from the Attorney General, it summoned Herbert K. Smith, the Head of the Bureau of Corporations, and requested the papers and documents on penalty of imprisonment for contempt. Mr. Smith reported the request to the President, who directed him to turn over to the President all the papers in the case "so that I could assist the Senate in the prosecution of its investigation." President Roosevelt then informed Senator Clark of the Judiciary Committee what had been done, that he had the papers and the only way the Senate could get them was through his impeachment. President Roosevelt also explained that some of the facts were given to the Government under the seal of secrecy and cannot be divulged, "and I will see to it that the word of this Government to the individual is kept sacred." (Corwin, *The President: Office and Powers,* pp. 281, 428; Abbott, *The Letters of Archie Butt, Personal Aid to President Roosevelt,* pp. 305–6.)

PRESIDENT COOLIDGE'S ADMINISTRATION

In 1924, during the administration of President Coolidge, the latter objected to the action of a special investigating committee appointed by the Senate to investigate the Bureau of Internal Revenue. Request was made by the committee for a list of the companies in which the Secretary of the Treasury was alleged to be interested for the purpose of investigating their tax returns. Calling this exercise of power an unwarranted intrusion, President Coolidge said:

"Whatever may be necessary for the information of the Senate or any of its committees in order to better enable them to perform their legislative or other constitutional functions ought always to be furnished willingly and expeditiously by any department. But it is recognized both by law and custom that there is certain confidential information which it would be detrimental to the public service to reveal" (68th Cong., 1st sess., *Record,* April 11, 1924, p. 6087).

PRESIDENT HOOVER'S ADMINISTRATION

A similar question arose in 1930 during the administration of President Hoover. Secretary of State Stimson refused to disclose to the Chairman of the Senate Foreign Relations Committee certain confidential telegrams and letters leading up to the London Conference and the London Treaty. The Committee asserted its right to have full and free access to all records touching the negotiations of the treaty, basing its right on the constitutional prerogative of the Senate in the treaty-making process. In his message to the Senate, President Hoover pointed out that there were a great many informal statements and reports which were given to the Government in confidence. The Executive was under a duty, in order to maintain amicable relations with other nations, not to publicize all the negotiations and statements which went into the making of the treaty. He further declared that the Executive must not be guilty of a breach of trust, nor violate the invariable practice of nations. "In view of this, I believe that to further comply with the above resolution would be incompatible with the public interest" (S. Doc. No. 216, 71st Cong., special sess., p. 2).

PRESIDENT FRANKLIN D. ROOSEVELT'S ADMINISTRATION

The position was followed during the administration of President Franklin D. Roosevelt. There were many instances in which the President and his Executive heads refused to make available certain information to Congress the disclosure of which was deemed to be confidential or contrary to the public interest. Merely a few need be cited.

1. Federal Bureau of Investigation records and reports were refused to congressional committees, in the public interest (40 Op. A. G. No. 8, April 30, 1941).

2. The Director of the Federal Bureau of Investigation refused to give testimony or to exhibit a copy of the President's directive requiring him, in the interests of national security, to refrain from testifying or from disclosing the contents of the Bureau's reports and activities. (*Hearings*, vol. 2, House, 78th Cong. Select Committee to Investigate the Federal Communications Commission, 1944, p. 2337.)

3. Communications between the President and the heads of departments were held to be confidential and privileged and not subject to inquiry by a committee of one of the Houses of Congress. (Letter dated January 22, 1944, signed Francis Biddle, Attorney General to Select Committee, etc.)

4. The Director of the Bureau of the Budget refused to testify and to produce the Bureau's files, pursuant to subpoena which had been served upon him, because the President had instructed him not to

make public the records of the Bureau due to their confidential nature. Public interest was again invoked to prevent disclosure. (Reliance placed on Attorney General's Opinion in 40 Op. A. G. No. 8, April 30, 1941.)

5. The Secretaries of War and Navy were directed not to deliver documents which the committee had requested, on grounds of public interest. The Secretaries, in their own judgment, refused permission to Army and Navy officers to appear and testify because they felt that it would be contrary to the public interests. (*Hearings*, Select Committee to Investigate the Federal Communications Commission, vol. 1, pp. 46, 48–68.)

PRESIDENT TRUMAN'S ADMINISTRATION

During the Truman administration also the President adhered to the traditional Executive view that the President's discretion must govern the surrender of Executive files. Some of the major incidents during the administration of President Truman in which information, records, and files were denied to Congressional Committees were as follows:

Date	Type of Document Refused
Mar. 4, 1948	FBI letter-report on Dr. Condon, Director of National Bureau of Standards, refused by Secretary of Commerce.
Mar. 15, 1948	President issued directive forbidding all Executive departments and agencies to furnish information or reports concerning loyalty of their employees to any court or committee of Congress, unless President approves.
March 1948	Dr. John R. Steelman, Confidential Adviser to the President, refused to appear before Committee on Education and Labor of the House, following the service of two subpoenas upon him. President directed him not to appear.
Aug. 5, 1948	Attorney General wrote Senator Ferguson, Chairman of Senate Investigations Subcommittee, that he would not furnish letters, memoranda, and other notices which the Justice Department had furnished to other government agencies concerning W. W. Remington.
Feb. 22, 1950	Senate Res. 231 directing Senate Subcommittee to procure State Department loyalty files was met with President Truman's refusal, following vigorous opposition of J. Edgar Hoover.

Mar. 27, 1950   Attorney General and Director of FBI appeared before Senate Subcommittee. Mr. Hoover's historic statement of reasons for refusing to furnish raw files approved by Attorney General.

May 16, 1951   General Bradley refused to divulge conversations between President and his advisers to combined Senate Foreign Relations and Armed Services Committees.

Jan. 31, 1952   President Truman directed Secretary of State to refuse to Senate Internal Security Subcommittee the reports and views of foreign service officers.

Apr. 22, 1952   Acting Attorney General Perlman laid down procedure for complying with requests for inspection of Department of Justice files by Committee on Judiciary:

> Requests on open cases would not be honored. Status report will be furnished.

> As to closed cases, files would be made available. All FBI reports and confidential information would not be made available.

> As to personnel files, they are never disclosed.

Apr. 3, 1952   President Truman instructed Secretary of State to withhold from Senate Appropriations Subcommittee files on loyalty and security investigations of employees—policy to apply to all Executive agencies. The names of individuals determined to be security risks would not be divulged. The voting record of members of an agency loyalty board would not be divulged.

Thus, you can see that the Presidents of the United States have withheld information of Executive departments or agencies whenever it was found that the information sought was confidential or that its disclosure would be incompatible with the public interest or jeopardize the safety of the Nation. The courts too have held that the question whether the production of the papers was contrary to the public interest was a matter for the Executive to determine.

By keeping the lines which separate and divide the three great branches of our Government clearly defined, no one branch has been able to encroach upon the powers of the other.

Upon this firm principle our country's strength, liberty, and democratic form of government will continue to endure.

APPENDIX B

Letters Regarding the Presidential Letter of May 17, 1954

October 9, 1956

Hon. DWIGHT D. EISENHOWER,
The President of the United States,
The White House, Washington, D.C.

DEAR MR. PRESIDENT: At your press conference on Thursday, September 27, 1956, you were asked whether your letter of May 17, 1954, to Secretary of Defense Charles E. Wilson was being misused as authority to restrict information from the public.

This question was posed by Mr. Clark Mollenhoff of the Des Moines Register and Tribune.

You stated that if Mr. Mollenhoff would put the question in writing —which I understand he has done—it will be answered.

This particular letter and its misuse by a number of Federal departments and agencies has been a great concern to the Special Subcommittee on Government Information. Although the letter, and the accompanying memorandum from the Attorney General, granted authority to one particular agency to refuse information to a specific committee of Congress in a single instance, 19 departments and agencies have cited the letter as authority to refuse information to the public or the Congress.

This occurred in agency answers to the subcommittee's questionnaire of November 7, 1955, on information practices and policies as well as during subcommittee hearings with executive officials.

Enclosed is an intermediate report, adopted unanimously by the House Government Operations Committee, on the subcommittee's study of restrictions on information. The problem of misuse of the May 17, 1954, letter is discussed on page 90 and at other points.

When the answer to Mr. Mollenhoff's question has been prepared and transmitted to him, the subcommittee would appreciate receiving copies of it and any other comments you have on the matter.

Respectfully,
JOHN E. MOSS, *Chairman*

THE WHITE HOUSE,
Washington, October 17, 1956.

Hon. JOHN E. MOSS,
House of Representatives, Washington, D.C.

DEAR MR. MOSS: This will acknowledge your October 9 letter to the President asking that you be supplied with copies of the answer to a question submitted by Mr. Clark Mollenhoff of the Des Moines Register and Tribune.

The answer to this question has not yet been given. However, as soon as it is, we will get in touch with you.

Sincerely,
GERALD D. MORGAN,
Special Counsel to the President

October 26, 1956

Mr. CLARK R. MOLLENHOFF,
Des Moines Register and Tribune,
National Press Building, Washington, D.C.

DEAR CLARK: At the press conference on September 27, 1956, you asked the President whether "all employees of the Federal Government, at their own discretion, can determine whether they will testify or will not testify before congressional committees when there is no security problem involved."

In the President's letter of May 17, 1954, to Secretary Wilson, the President set forth the general principles that are to govern all employees in the executive branch concerning their testimony, or the production of documents, relating to their conversations or communications with, or their advice to, each other on official matters. In his press conference of July 6, 1955, the President further amplified the principles set forth in this letter as follows:

"If anybody in an official position of this Government does anything which is an official act, and submits it either in the form of recommendation or anything else, that is properly a matter for investigation if Congress so chooses, provided the national security is not involved.

"But when it comes to the conversations that take place between any responsible official and his advisers, or exchange of mere little slips, of this or that, expressing personal opinions on the most confidential basis, those are not subject to investigation by anybody. And if they are it will wreck the Government."

In so writing to Secretary Wilson, and in further amplifying these principles, the President was exercising a right, which is his, and his alone, to determine what action is necessary to maintain the proper separation of powers between the executive and legislative branches of the Government. In the orderly administration of the Government, the head of each executive agency directs the manner in which these principles are enforced.

The underlying reasons for these principles are set forth in the President's letter of May 17, 1954. It is essential to efficient and effective administration that employees of the executive branch be in a position to be completely candid in advising each other on official matters. It is essential, if channels of information are to be kept open, that confidences among employees should not be breached.

It will continue to be this administration's policy to keep the Congress and the people fully informed of what is being done in the executive branch. An employee is not free merely to exercise his own discretion but in the final analysis information will be withheld only when the President or agency heads acting under the President's authority or instruction determine it is contrary to the public interest to disclose it.

All of the above, of course, is subject to the Executive order dealing with the classification of information in the interest of security, and to the various statutes and regulations of the department and agencies relating to information to be held in confidence.

I hope this answers your inquiry.

Sincerely,
GERALD D. MORGAN,
Special Counsel to the President

APPENDIX C

Correspondence on the Right of Access to Information by the General Accounting Office

November 12, 1958

Hon. DWIGHT D. EISENHOWER,
President of the United States,
Washington, D.C.

DEAR MR. PRESIDENT: I just returned to Washington for a hearing of the Government Information Subcommittee. The subcommittee, I understand, will inquire into the matter of General Accounting Office access to Air Force Inspector General's reports. In that context, my attention has been directed to your press conference comments of November 5, and to some newspaper speculation about those comments.

The text of your remarks to which I refer is as follows:

"Q. (Clark R. Mollenhoff, Des Moines Register). Mr. President, you have mentioned the spending in the Defense Department here as one of the important issues, and the General Accounting Office, which is the watchdog on frauds and extravagance in the various agencies, has been barred from reports over in the Air Force and the Defense Department generally, and on this they claim that they have authority from you to withhold reports any time it is 'inexpedient to do so.'

"I wonder if you have given that authority and if you feel that the GAO should have a full rein to go in and investigate all indications of fraud and extravagance.

"The PRESIDENT. You are obviously talking about some special thing that I would have to study before I could make—give an answer.

"I have stated this time and again: I believe that every investigating committee of the Congress, every auditing office, like the GAO, should always have an opportunity to see official records if the security of our country is not involved.

"Q. (Clark R. Mollenhoff, Des Moines Register). Well, they claim this, Mr. President, under executive privilege.

"The PRESIDENT. No, that's all I have to say—I told you that is all I had to say for the moment."

While this question-and-answer exchange did not identify Inspector General reports, and while you did preface your comment by saying this obviously referred to some special thing you would have to study before giving an answer, I would nevertheless like to ask this: Did you mean to imply by your comments that the complete text of Inspector General reports, including recommendations, be made available to Congress and the General Accounting Office?

Respectfully,
CLARE E. HOFFMAN

THE WHITE HOUSE
Washington, November 12, 1958.

Hon. CLARE E. HOFFMAN,
House of Representatives, Washington, D.C.

DEAR MR. HOFFMAN: Thank you for your letter inquiring about comments in my November 5 press conference.

I believe, of course, that the public, the Congress, and such auditing units as the General Accounting Office should have all the information departments and agencies can properly make available. However, the public interest also demands order and efficiency in the operation of these departments and agencies. And in my judgment the public interest is not necessarily served by divulging the advice, suggestions, or recommendations which subordinate employees periodically make to their superiors. In this connection, recommendations of inspectors general have been a most useful advisory tool in administering the military departments; and historically, recommendations and other advisory matter in such reports have not been released. I think this practice is a correct one, and is in the best interest of the Nation. At the same time, I want to add that the facts are distinct from advice and recommendations in these reports. It is my understanding that all the facts developed in the inspector general's report to which you refer are being made available at the request of the General Accounting Office.

Sincerely,
DWIGHT D. EISENHOWER

UNITED STATES GENERAL ACCOUNTING OFFICE,
OFFICE OF GENERAL COUNSEL,
Washington, D.C., November 4, 1958.

MEMORANDUM ON RIGHT OF THE COMPTROLLER GENERAL TO ACCESS TO A REPORT OF THE INSPECTOR GENERAL OF THE AIR FORCE ENTITLED "SURVEY OF MANAGEMENT OF THE BALLISTIC MISSILES PROGRAM"

The basic statutory authority of the Comptroller General for access to records of departments and agencies is set forth in section 313 of the Budget and Accounting Act, 1921 (31 U.S.C. 54). Section 313 provides:

"*All departments and establishments shall furnish to the Comptroller General such information* regarding the powers, duties, activities, organization, financial transactions, and methods of business of their respective offices *as he may* from time to time *require of them;* and the Comptroller General, or any of his assistants or employees, when duly authorized by him, shall, for the purpose of securing such information, have access to and the right to examine *any* books, documents, papers, or records of *any* such department or establishment. The authority contained in this section shall not be applicable to expenditures made under the provisions of section 291 of the Revised Statutes."

It will be noted that the only exception in section 313 relates to expenditures made under section 291, Revised Statutes (31 U.S.C. 107), which authorizes the Secretary of State to account for certain confidential expenditures in connection with intercourse or treaties with foreign nations by certificate where, in his judgment, he may think it advisable not to specify the details of such expenditure. Since that is the only exception stated and following the legal maxim that the specific setting forth of one type of exception precludes others from arising, it seems clear that the Comptroller General may require, and the departments are required to furnish, documents, etc., as to any other transaction or activity. Also, the language of section 313 itself [except as to the expenditures under 291 R. S.] in requiring the departments to furnish such information as the Comptroller General "may require of them" and its requirement that he be *given access to any* documents of the departments, clearly gives him access to *all* such documentation. If he has access to *any* document, he has access to *all*. The legislative background of the Budget and Accounting Act, 1921, makes no qualification as to what records can be required; the provision itself apparently being considered sufficiently specific. The legislative reports do bring out that one of the principal functions of the Comptroller General is to enable the Congress to be kept advised as to expenditures of the Government, and that the Comptroller General is expected to criticize extravagance, duplication, and inefficiency in executive departments. There is no doubt, in passing the act, the Congress did not intend that the executive agencies could, or would, withhold any books, documents, papers, or records needed by the Comptroller General. Otherwise, the very purpose of the act would be nullified.

The authority and duty of the Comptroller General was amplified by section 206 of the Legislative Reorganization Act of 1946 (31 U.S.C. 60), which authorized and directed him to make expenditure analyses of each agency in the executive branch of the Government which "will enable Congress to determine whether public funds have been economically and efficiently administered and expended" and to make reports thereon from time to time to the Committees on Government Operations, and Appropriations and other committees having jurisdiction over legislation relating to the operation of the agencies involved. The work of the Comptroller General, together with the activities of the Committees on Government Operations, were to serve as a check on the economy and efficiency of administrative management. See pages 6 and 7, Senate Report No. 1400 on the Legislative Reorganization Act of 1946.

The Congress has also directed that the Comptroller General in performing his duties give full consideration to the administrative reports and controls of the departments and agencies. The Government Corporation Control Act specifically provides in section 301 (a) (31 U.S.C. 866), "That in making the audits . . . the Comptroller General shall, to the fullest extent deemed by him to be practicable, utilize reports of examination of Government corporations made by a supervising administrative agency pursuant to law." The legislative reports on that act, Senate Report 694, page 10, contains the following significant language:

"The audit provisions are intended to give the Congress the independent audit reports of its agent, the Comptroller General, as to the operations and financial condition of every Government corporation in which the Government has a capital interest. . . . If the audit by the Comptroller General is to be a truly independent audit, he must not be restricted in such a way as to prevent him from examining into and reporting the transactions of any Government corporation to the extent deemed by him to be necessary.

"The Comptroller General has stated that in making his audits he will give full consideration to the effectiveness of the existing systems of internal accounts, procedures, and controls and of external examinations by an administrative supervisory agency. The bill includes a specific provision requiring the Comptroller General in making his audits to utilize, to the fullest extent deemed by him to be practicable, reports of examinations of Government corporations by a supervising administrative agency pursuant to law."

The Budget and Accounting Procedures Act of 1950 requires each executive agency to maintain systems of accounting and internal control and provides, in section 117 (a) (31 U.S.C. 67 [a]), that the Comptroller General in determining auditing procedures and the extent of examination to be given accounts and vouchers give consideration to "the effectiveness of accounting organizations and systems, internal audit and control, and related administrative practices of the respective agencies."

The Comptroller General is required to audit the activities of the executive departments and agencies; to make expenditure analyses to determine whether funds have economically been expended; and to give consideration to the departments' internal audit and control and related administrative practices. To perform these duties he is given the clear statutory authority to require information of the departments and agencies regarding their organization, activities, and methods of business, coupled with the right to access to *any* books, documents, papers, or records of any such establishment (except as to the confidential State Department funds).

There have been no court cases construing the statutes giving the Comptroller General access to records. However, in 1925, the Attorney General in an opinion to the Secretary of War (34 Op. Atty. Gen. 446), concerning a request by the Comptroller General for information relative to an award of a contract showing that the lowest bid was accepted, or if otherwise, a statement for the reasons for accepting other than the lowest bid, advised, in part, as follows:

"It will be observed that the Comptroller General states that this requirement is made necessary in order that a satisfactory audit may be made. What papers or data he should have to make such an audit would seem to be a matter solely for his determination. Moreover, section 313 of the Budget and Accounting Act provides (p. 26):

"All departments and establishments shall furnish to the Comptroller

General such information regarding the powers, duties, activities, organization, financial transactions, and methods of business of their respective offices as he may from time to time require of them; and the Comptroller General, or any of his assistants or employees, when duly authorized by him, shall, for the purpose of securing such information, have access to and the right to examine any books, documents, papers, or records of any such department or establishment. . . ."

Questions as to whether the General Accounting Office has a right to access to records claimed to be confidential for security or other reasons have arisen from time to time and the General Accounting Office has always taken the position that it has the right to the information, even though certain provisions of law relating to disclosure might be applicable to it.

The General Accounting Office recognizes that certain of the functions of the inspectors general, such as criminal and personnel investigations, are of a confidential nature and it will normally accept summaries of facts contained in such reports to the extent they are needed in connection with its work. However, the inspectors general also have as a part of their respective missions and duties responsibility for conducting inspections, surveys, and examinations of the effectiveness of operations and overall efficiency of a command, installation, or activity. These functions may be performed on a periodic or special basis as directed by competent authority. The performance of these functions constitutes an important part of the process of management evaluations and internal reviews as distinguished from criminal or personnel investigations. They provide officials and appropriate personnel of authority with an independent appraisal of the effectiveness of operations and overall efficiency. Moreover, a very considerable part of the inspections and reviews made by the inspectors general involve reviews of procedures and policies and as such are an important segment of the internal reviews and control which the General Accounting Office, under section 117 (a) of the Budget and Accounting Procedures Act of 1950 is required to consider and recognize in determining the audit procedures to be followed in its reviews.

The scope of inspection and survey programs of the inspectors general is similar in character to much of the work the General Accounting Office has scheduled in requirements, procurement, supply management, and research and development areas. The programs of the Deputy Inspector General for Inspection of the Air Force covering the period July 1, to December 31, 1958, include (1) a survey of Air Force procurement methods (advertising versus negotiation); (2) a survey of procurement quantitative and qualitative program changes; (3) a survey of procurement of commercial communications and utility services; (4) a survey of contract cost overruns; (5) a survey of maintenance programs; (6) a survey of modification programs; (7)

a survey of the application of electronic data processing systems and other like subjects. All of these subjects represent internal and management evaluations which would clearly be a part of "internal audit and control" within the meaning of section 117 (a) of the Accounting and Auditing Act of 1950. It is essential that such reports be made available to the General Accounting Office in order that it can evaluate the effectiveness of the department's system of internal control and to preclude unwarranted and unnecessary duplication of effort in the internal audit and the independent review made by this Office. The Air Force Inspector General's report on the ballistic missiles program clearly falls within the term "internal audit and control."

The Secretary of the Air Force in refusing the Comptroller General access to the Inspector General's report on the ballistic missiles program stated that the Inspector General's reports are prepared solely for the use of responsible officials within the Air Force, and that the objective of self-criticism can be obtained only if the Inspector General's organization has the assurance that its reports will, without exception, be kept within the Department. The Secretary also stated that the report in question concerned the internal management of the Department, and was prepared solely for the benefit and use of those officers and employees of the Department who are responsible for its administration, and that the release of such reports to persons outside the Department would have a serious effect on the effective administration of the Department. The Secretary concluded that these considerations compelled him to conclude that the public interest would best be served by not releasing the report.

It is our understanding that the position of the Secretary is premised on paragraph 151 (b) (3) of the Manual for Courts Martial (1951) which was prescribed by the President on February 8, 1951, through Executive Order 10214, pursuant to the act of May 5, 1950 (64 Stat. 107), and on the general basis that the heads of executive departments have the right to withhold information or papers which they deem confidential, in the public interest.

The Manual for Courts Martial, 1951, Executive Order 10214, dated February 8, 1951, was issued pursuant to article 36 of the act of May 5, 1950 (64 Stat. 120). Article 36 (a) provides:

"The procedure, including modes of proof, in cases before courts-martial, courts of inquiry, military commissions, and other military tribunals may be prescribed by the President by regulations which shall, so far as he deems practicable, apply the principles of law and the rules of evidence generally recognized in the trial of criminal cases in the United States district courts, but which shall not be contrary or inconsistent with this code."

Article 151 (b) (3) of the Manual for Courts Martial provides: "The Inspectors General of the various armed forces, and their assistants, are confidential agents of the Secretaries of the military or executive departments concerned, or of the military commander on whose staff they may be serving. Their investigations are privileged unless a different procedure is prescribed by the authority ordering the investigation. Reports of such investigations and their accompanying testimony and exhibits are likewise privileged, and there is no authority of law or practice requiring that copies thereof be furnished to any person other than the authority ordering the investigation or superior authority. However, when application is made to the authority by court-martial certain testimony, or an exhibit, accompanying a report of investigation, which testimony or exhibit has become material in a trial (to show an inconsistent statement of a witness, for example), he should ordinarily approve such application unless the testimony or exhibit requested contains a state secret or unless in the exercise of a sound discretion he is of the opinion that it would be contrary to public policy to divulge the information desired.

"In certain cases, it may become necessary to introduce evidence of a highly confidential or secret nature, as when an accused is on trial for having unlawfully communicated information of such a nature to persons not entitled thereto. In a case of this type, the court should take adequate precautions to insure that no greater dissemination of such evidence occurs than the necessities of the trial require. The courtroom should be cleared of spectators while such evidence is being received or commented upon, and all persons whose duties require them to remain should be warned that they are not to communicate such confidential or secret information. . . ."

Since the Manual for Courts Martial was issued pursuant to the authority of the President to prescribe procedure for such trials, and Article 151 (b) MCM by its language is addressed to procedures of such courts, it obviously does not affect access by the General Accounting Office to Inspector General's reports determined by the Comptroller General to be necessary to the performance of his work, particularly where the report requested is not one dealing with personnel or criminal investigations.

Air Force Regulation 120–3, paragraph 9, October 11, 1954, and similar regulations provide:

"Disclosure of or access to matters pertinent to an inquiry or investigation will be limited to persons whose official duties require such knowledge. The Manual for Courts Martial, 1951, states that inspector-general investigations are privileged information. The same privileged status applies to inquiries and investigations conducted under this Regulation. Also paragraph 3, AFR 190–16, 29 July 1954, excludes investigative reports and reports of inspectors general and base inspectors from release to the public as information. Reports by investigators will not be released or disclosed outside the Air Force without approval of the Secretary of the Air Force."

Presumably these regulations were issued pursuant to section 161, Revised Statutes, title 5, United States Code, section 22, or similar authority, authorizing the head of a department to issue regulations, *not inconsistent with law,* for the conduct of his department and the custody and use of its records. Since under section 313 of the Budget and Accounting Act the Secretary is required to give the Comptroller General access to the records, any construction of the Air Force regulation denying the Comptroller General access is improper, and the regulation to that extent, being inconsistent with law, has no effect.

With reference to the right or privilege of the head of the "Executive" branch of the Government to refuse to the legislative and judicial branch of the Government free access to records in the custody of the executive departments, support for such claim of right or privilege is found in 25 Op. Atty. Gen. 326, 40 Op. Atty. Gen. 45, and cases referred to therein.

Assuming, arguendo, that such right or privilege does exist, we do not believe it warrants an executive agency denying to the Comptroller General information or access to its documents in view of section 313 of the Budget and Accounting Act which clearly provides that "all departments . . . shall furnish . . . information . . ." required by the Comptroller General and that he shall have "access to and the right to examine any . . . documents of any such department. . . ." The opinion of the Attorney General in 1925, 34 Op. Atty. Gen. 446, discussed earlier, clearly recognizes the prerogative of the Comptroller General to determine what papers he should have to enable him properly to perform his audits and that the departments are required to furnish them.

The right or privilege asserted from time to time by the executive branch was considered in a study by the staff of the House Committee on Government Operations entitled "The right of Congress to obtain information from the Executive and from other agencies of the Federal Government," committee print dated May 3, 1956, and in great detail by the House Committee on Government Operations in connection with Public Law 85–619 approved August 12, 1958, as were the court cases cited and relied upon by the Attorney General. See House Report No. 1461, 85th Congress, 2d session. Also, there was there considered a line of later decisions starting with *McGrain* v. *Daugherty,* 273 U. S. 135 (1927) which upheld the power of Congress to require information sought for legislative purposes. None of the cases relied upon by the Attorney General involved demands by the Congress for information from the executive agencies. This was considered in a study on the matter furnished the committee by the Attorney General. See page 2938 of the printed hearings before a subcommittee of the House Committee on Government Operations on June 20 and 22, 1956, on "Availability of Information from Federal Departments and Agencies" wherein after citing and quoting from numerous court decisions he stated "None of the foregoing cases involved the refusal by a head of department to obey a call for papers or information. There has been no Supreme Court decision dealing squarely with that question."

As indicated, the precise question of whether the Congress has a right to obtain information from the Executive which it refuses to furnish because of its confidential nature has not been the subject of a court decision. Where information sought by Congress by an executive department has been refused, the Congress has, at times, succeeded in bringing sufficient pressure to bear to obtain the information, or the executive department has, upon reconsideration, relented and furnished it. At other times the Congress has not pressed the matter—possibly because of its feeling that the President was in such a position that he should know whether the information should be withheld, or that the Congress had no machinery to force his compliance—and the information was not furnished. But, regardless of whether such right or privilege exists, it is clear that the Congress in passing on future appropriations and other legislation has a right to know whether the funds appropriated are being properly and efficiently used for the purposes it intended and that any information available in that regard should be available to the Comptroller General.

In view of the above, and in the absence of any judicial determination specifically dealing with the rights of the Comptroller General under section 313, we do not believe that the position of the Secretary of the Air Force that the report in question can be legally withheld is proper.

ROBERT F. KELLER, *General Counsel*

Letter from the Attorney General to the President

December 22, 1960

The PRESIDENT,
The White House.

DEAR MR. PRESIDENT: You have requested my advice whether, under the Constitution and laws of the United States, you have the authority as Chief Executive to issue the two attached directives to, respectively, the Secretary of State and the Secretary of the Treasury, concerning the availability of mutual security program funds for the expenses of the Office of the Inspector General and Comptroller established under section 533A of the Mutual Security Act of 1954, as amended.

In an opinion I have furnished you at your request, I have advised you of my conclusions that: First, the view taken by the Comptroller General in his letter of December 8, 1960, that the proviso contained in section 533A(d) of the Mutual Security Act of 1954, as amended, has operated to cut off the funds here in question, is erroneous. Second, that if this view of the Comptroller General as to the meaning of the proviso is correct, the proviso is unconstitutional. Third, that therefore, despite the Comptroller General's letters of December 8, 1960, and December 13, 1960, these mutual security program funds continue to be available as heretofore for the expenses of the Office of the Inspector General and Comptroller. The reasons for these conclusions are set forth at length in my opinion.

Your directives to the Secretaries of State and the Treasury are, you advise me, in your judgment desirable to insure that mutual security program funds will be available until the end of your term of office on January 20, 1961, as heretofore for the expenses of the Office of the Inspector General and Comptroller. Under these circumstances, I am of the opinion that you, as Chief Executive, have the authority to issue the directives.

Respectfully,
WILLIAM P. ROGERS,
Attorney General

Opinion of the Attorney General of the United States Dated December 19, 1960

MUTUAL SECURITY PROGRAM—CUTOFF OF FUNDS FROM
OFFICE OF INSPECTOR GENERAL AND COMPTROLLER

Section 533A(d) of the Mutual Security Act of 1954 added by section 401(h) of the Mutual Security Act of 1959 (73 Stat. 253), which directs that the expenses of the Office of the Inspector General and Comptroller with respect to programs under the Mutual Security Act be charged to the appropriations made to carry out such programs, *provided* that all documents, reports, and other materials relating to the operations and activities of that Office are furnished upon request to the General Accounting Office, or to any appropriate congressional committee or duly authorized subcommittee, does not authorize the funds of the Office of the Inspector General and Comptroller to be cut off because of the failure of the State Department to furnish certain documents relating to that Office to a congressional subcommittee, if the President has issued a certificate pursuant to section 101(d) of the Mutual Security and Related Agencies Appropriation Act, 1961 (74 Stat. 778), to the effect that he has forbidden the production of those documents and states his reasons for so doing. A contrary conclusion reached by the Comptroller General is incorrect, and, therefore, funds continue to be available as heretofore for the Office of the Inspector General and Comptroller.

The proviso in section 533A(d) does not expressly authorize the funds of the Office of the Inspector General and Comptroller to be cut off, and such a drastic consequence should not lightly be inferred from ambiguous statutory language. Other provisions of the Mutual Security Act of 1959, the Mutual Security Act of 1960 (74 Stat. 134), the Mutual Security and Related Agencies Appropriation Act, 1960 (73 Stat. 717), and the Mutual Security and Related Agencies Appropriation Act, 1961, indicate a congressional purpose not to compel the disclosure of information concerning the mutual security program which the President considers to be incompatible with the security of the United States. Section 533A(d) should be read in the light of this purpose.

Section 533A(d) has been suspended by section 101(d) of the Mutual Security and Related Agencies Appropriation Act, 1961, which provides that the failure to furnish documents, etc., to Congress or to the Comptroller General will not result in a cutoff of appropriated funds if the President certifies that he has prohibited the production of the documents and states the reasons for this action.

A construction of the proviso to section 533A(d), requiring funds for the Office of the Inspector General and Comptroller to be cut off for failure to supply documents, notwithstanding the President's certification, must be avoided because it not only creates constitutional doubts, but would, if correct, render the proviso unconstitutional. Congress cannot by direct action compel the President to furnish to it information the disclosure of which he considers contrary to the national interest. It cannot achieve this result indirectly by placing a condition upon the expenditure of appropriated funds.

APPENDIX D

*Letter from President Kennedy
to the Secretary of Defense*

February 8, 1962

DEAR MR. SECRETARY: You have brought to my attention the fact that the Senate's Special Preparedness Investigating Subcommittee intends to ask witnesses from your department to give testimony identifying the names of individuals who made or recommended changes in specific speeches.

As you know, it has been and will be the consistent policy of this administration to cooperate fully with the committees of the Congress with respect to the furnishing of information. In accordance with this policy, you have made available to the subcommittee 1500 speeches with marginal notes, hundreds of other documents and the names of the fourteen individual speech reviewers, eleven of whom are military officers. You have also made available the fullest possible background information about each of these men, whose record of service and devotion to the country is unquestioned in every case; and you have permitted the committee staff to interview all witnesses requested and to conduct such interviews outside the presence of any departmental representative. Finally, you have identified the departmental source of each suggested change, and offered to furnish in writing an explanation of each such change, and the policy or guideline under which it was made.

Your statement that these changes are your responsibility, that they were made under your policies and guidelines and those of this administration and that you would be willing to explain them in detail, is both fitting and accurate, and offers to the subcommittee all the information properly needed for purposes of its current inquiry. It is equally clear that it would not be possible for you to maintain an orderly department, and receive the candid advice and loyal respect of your subordinates, if they—instead of you and your senior associates—are to be individually answerable to the Congress as well as to you for their internal acts and advice.

For these reasons, and in accordance with the precedents on separation of powers established by my predecessors from the first to the last, I have concluded that it would be contrary to the public interest to make available any information which would enable the subcommittee to identify and hold accountable any individual with respect to any particular speech that he has reviewed. I therefore direct you, and all personnel under the jurisdiction of your department, not to give any testimony or produce any documents which would disclose such information; and I am issuing parallel instructions to the Secretary of State.

The principle which is at stake here cannot be automatically applied to every request for information. Each case must be judged on its own merits. But I do not intend to permit subordinate officials of our career services to bear the brunt of congressional inquiry into policies which are the responsibilities of their superiors.

Sincerely yours,
JOHN F. KENNEDY

APPENDIX E

Executive Privilege Correspondence between President Kennedy and Congressman John E. Moss

February 15, 1962

The Honorable
John F. Kennedy
The President of the United States
The White House
Washington, D.C.

Dear Mr. President:

In your letter of February 8, 1962 to Secretary McNamara you directed him to refuse certain information to a Senate Subcommittee. The concluding paragraph of your letter stated:

> "The principle which is at stake here cannot be automatically applied to every request for information. Each case must be judged on its merits."

A similar letter from President Eisenhower on May 17, 1954 also refused information to a Senate Subcommittee, setting forth the same arguments covered in your letter. President Eisenhower did not, however, state that future questions of availability of information to the Congress would have to be answered as they came up.

I know you are aware of the result of President Eisenhower's letter.

Time after time Executive Branch employees far down the administrative line from the President fell back on his letter of May 17, 1954
as authority to withhold information from the Congress and the public.

Some of the cases are well known—the Dixon-Yates matter and the
investigation of East-West trade controls, for instance—but many of the
refusals based on President Eisenhower's letter of May 17, 1954 received no public notice. A report of the House Committee on Government Operations covering the five years from June, 1955 through June,
1960 lists 44 cases of Executive Branch officials refusing information
on the basis of the principles set forth in the May 17, 1954 letter.

I am confident that you share my belief that your letter of February
8, 1962 to Secretary McNamara should not be seized upon by Executive Branch employees—many of them holding the same policy-making
positions of responsibility they did under the Eisenhower Administration—as a new claim of authority to withhold information from the
Congress and the public. A Subcommittee staff study indicates that
during the year between the time you took office and February 8,
1962 the claim of an "executive privilege" to withhold government
information was not used successfully once, compared to the dozens of
times in previous years administrative employees held up "executive
privilege" as a shield against public and Congressional access to information.

Although your letter of February 8, 1962 stated clearly that the
principle involved could not be applied automatically to restrict information, this warning received little public notice. Clarification of this
point would, I believe, serve to prevent the rash of restrictions on government information which followed the May 17, 1954 letter from
President Eisenhower.

Sincerely,
/s/ John E. Moss
Chairman

THE WHITE HOUSE
Washington

March 7, 1962

Dear Mr. Chairman:
This is in reply to your letter of last month inquiring generally about
the practice this Administration will follow in invoking the doctrine
of executive privilege in withholdng certain information from the
Congress.

As your letter indicated, my letter of February 8 to Secretary Mc-
Namara made it perfectly clear that the directive to refuse to make
certain specific information available to a special subcommittee of the

Senate Armed Services Committee was limited to that specific request and that "each case must be judged on its merits."

As you know, this Administration has gone to great lengths to achieve full cooperation with the Congress in making available to it all appropriate documents, correspondence and information. That is the basic policy of this Administration, and it will continue to be so. Executive privilege can be invoked only by the President and will not be used without specific Presidential approval. Your own interest in assuring the widest public accessibility to governmental information is, of course, well known, and I can assure you this Administration will continue to cooperate with your subcommittee and the entire Congress in achieving this objective.

Sincerely,
/s/ JOHN F. KENNEDY

Honorable John E. Moss
Chairman
Special Government Information
   Subcommittee of the Committee
   on Government Operations
House of Representatives
Washington, D.C.